# AFTER NARCISSISTIC ABUSE

Surviving and Thriving after NPD abuse.
Recover from a toxic relationship.
How to reclaim your emotional life and true-self and ensuring you'll never get abused again.

DR.RACHEL BANCROFT PSYD

## © Copyright 2019 - All rights reserved.

The content contained within this book may not be reproduced, duplicated or transmitted without direct written permission from the author or the publisher.

Under no circumstances will any blame or legal responsibility be held against the publisher, or author, for any damages, reparation, or monetary loss due to the information contained within this book. Either directly or indirectly.

**Legal Notice:**

This book is copyright protected. This book is only for personal use. You cannot amend, distribute, sell, use, quote or paraphrase any part, or the content within this book, without the consent of the author or publisher.

**Disclaimer Notice:**

Please note the information contained within this document is for educational and entertainment purposes only. All effort has been executed to present accurate, up to date, and reliable, complete information. No warranties of any kind are declared or implied. Readers acknowledge that the author is not engaging in the rendering of legal, financial, medical or professional advice. The content within this book has been derived from various sources. Please consult a licensed professional before attempting any techniques outlined in this book.

By reading this document, the reader agrees that under no circumstances is the author responsible for any losses, direct or indirect, which are incurred as a result of the use of information contained within this document, including, but not limited to, — errors, omissions, or inaccuracies.

INTRODUCTION .................................................................................. 6

PART I UNDERSTANDING NARCISSISM ........................................... 9

What Is a Narcissist? ........................................................................ 9

The Disappearing act ..................................................................... 15

A Narcissist's Strategy ................................................................... 17

Example Of Covert Narcissism ...................................................... 18

The Contrast between Male and Female Narcissists ................... 21

Healthy Narcissism ........................................................................ 24

Nature VS nurture ......................................................................... 27

PART II COMMON MYTHS ABOUT NARCISSISM ......................... 31

PART III TREATMENT FOR NARCISSISTIC BEHAVIOUR ................ 39

Cognitive Therapy ......................................................................... 40

Schema Therapy ............................................................................ 41

Foundations of Security: Biology and Attachment ...................... 47

PART V HEALING AND RECOVERY ................................................ 50

The Effects Of Narcissistic Behaviour ........................................... 50

Four Stages of Transformation ..................................................... 54

Boundaries .................................................................................... 56

Strategies and Control .................................................................. 58

Typical Emotional Responses ....................................................... 60

## PART V TIPS AND TRICKS THAT AID RECOVERY .................................. 63

Mindfulness .................................................................................................. 63

The Four Masks of the Narcissist and How to Deal with Them .................. 75

Exercise For Emotional Triggers .................................................................. 81

Recognising Your Own Pitfalls ..................................................................... 83

## PART VI COMFORT ZONES: ........................................................... 85

## THE TRIALS OF LIVING WITH AND REMODELLING YOUR HABITS ...... 85

Reasons the Narcissist Triggers You ........................................................... 86

Cultivating an Authentic Voice .................................................................... 88

The Ability to Discover and Transform ....................................................... 90

## PART VII EMPATHY .......................................................................... 92

The difference between Empathy and Sympathy ...................................... 93

Feeling "Sensed" .......................................................................................... 95

A Brief Glimpse at the Science of Empathy ................................................ 98

Deep Within ............................................................................................... 101

Retaining the Narcissist on the Hook ....................................................... 103

The Role of Empathy in the Therapeutic Relationship ............................ 105

## PART VIII NEW FORMS OF COMMUNICATION
## WITH A NARCISSIST ........................................................................ 109

Harnessing the Force ................................................................................ 110

Presenting Your Offerings ......................................................................... 112

The Seven Artful Forms Of Communication ...... 114

## PART IX ESCAPING PERILOUS NARCISSISM ...... 123

Identifying Dangerous Narcissism ...... 124

Constant justifications ...... 125

Reforming the Average Narcissist ...... 129

# Introduction

Narcissism. We no longer have to look too far to find it. It's become an epidemic.

People nowadays acquire expensive homes with lending facilities given to them by banks that far exceed their current income.

Teenagers continuously strive to package themselves as a product to be sold by creating their own "personal brand".

Students verbally abuse and beat their classmates, proceeding to seek attention and validation by posting videos of these behaviours to social networks such as Youtube.

These may seem like a collection of current cultural trends, but all are rooted in the underlying change in our cultural and societal psychology.

Not only are there more narcissist than ever documented before, but non-narcissistic people are continually being seduced by the ever-growing emphasis on material and capitalistic wealth, celebrity adoration, and appearance.

Wants and needs have shifted, consuming otherwise humble individuals into the belief system of marble kitchen countertops, beauty-enhancing surgery, and bogus social media profiles.

The growth of narcissism is accelerating at an exponentially alarming rate.

In 2006, 1 out of 4 students agreed with a vast majority of the details on a regulatory measure of narcissistic traits.

The more severe clinically diagnosed version of the trait, Narcissistic Personality Disorder, is also becoming far more widespread than before.

Approximately 1 out of 10 students in their twenties and 1 out of 16 of those of other ages have encountered the symptoms of NPD.

Similarly, to the current obesity epidemic, narcissism has not affected everyone in the same way. There are larger amounts of people that are obese, and consequentially there are more people who are narcissistic, but that doesn't negate the fact that there are still individuals that eat well and exercise, and those who are caring and loving.

Even the non-narcissistic have played witness to narcissistic behaviour online or through real-life interactions.
As an example, the financial crisis in 2008 was perpetuated and partly caused by the narcissistic behaviour of buyers who pretended they could afford homes far out of their price range, and self-centred lending institutions that played and took gambles with other people's finances.
So, whether it be in one way or another, it's clear to see that narcissism has touched nearly everyone.

Understanding the reason behind the growth in narcissism is important because its longterm effects are seriously detrimental to society.
Our current cultures focus on self-admiration has created a lack of grasp from reality;
We adore fake celebrities that have created success for themselves via egotistically posting their versions of reality to social media networks.
We praise fake geniuses with inflated grades due to backhanded payment plans.
We admire fake rich individuals who have countless amounts of debt and interest-only mortgages.
We praise appearance, and fake beauty achieved via cosmetic procedures and botulism.
And, we normalise fake friends and relationships because of the disassociation caused by the internet explosion and social media takeover.

Although all these fantasies feel good, reality unfortunately always prevails.

Celebrity worship has grown, reality TV has become an exhibition of narcissistic people, parenting has become permissive, the internet has created the opportunity of overnight fame and self-absorbed behaviour, furthermore the over availability of credit has conceded the means for people to fake their finances, all while the utilisation of a harmful toxin, botox, has been validated by society to prevent the signs of ageing and maintain appearances.

Narcissism leads to countless negative behaviours such as aggression, heightened materialism, lack of empathy, and zero values. And by striving to achieve a society that has extraordinary amounts of self-esteem and self-expression, we've actually allowed and created a culture that brings out narcissistic behaviour in all of us.

# PART I UNDERSTANDING NARCISSISM

It has been stated by many authorities in the field of psychotherapy that there are few challenges greater than treating a narcissist.
This is someone that has finally resorted to therapy because a partner courageously gave them an ultimatum, or an employer presented them with a final warning after countless behavioural complaints.
Perhaps they got involved in a legal matter and believe counselling will appear advantageous on their file.
And, on fewer occasions, moreover reluctantly, narcissists resort to therapy because they are depressed, anxious or lonely.

Although these characters seem self-assured and confident, they can abruptly pull the rug out from under, reducing you to trepidation, tears, antipathy, and boredom. These varieties of people are referred to as narcissists.

To correctly understand what is truly going on in your relationship with someone experiencing Narcissistic Personality Disorder, we must first dive deeply into the underlying root of the disease.

## What Is a Narcissist?

The word "narcissism" originates from Greek mythology's tale of Narcissus, who was doomed to forever be in love with his reflection in a mountain pool, as retribution for declining to accept a proposal of love from Echo, a mountain nymph.

Since Narcissus could only desire but never truly possess the reflection he saw in the pool, he quietly pined away and was ultimately transformed into a gorgeous flower.
The thought-provoking misfortune in this myth presents the moral that authentic lovability and beauty blossom when obsessive self- love perishes.

Narcissists are usually self-obsessed and consumed with a need to obtain the perfect image or status, and they have a decreased capacity for caring, listening, or empathising with others.
This level of self-absorption obstructs intimate and authentic connections.
Such relationships allow us to experience the contrast between self-love and love for another.
Mastering the balancing act between self-directed attention and other-directed is a crucial part of childhood, and it is considered a basic foundational tutorial for life; encouraging the understanding of responsibility, reciprocity and empathy toward others.

Unfortunately, this important learning curve is greatly lacking in the narcissist's initial development.

The narcissist may venture through life perpetuating a boastful ego, while subconsciously craving, like most of us, the safe and quiet sanctuary found within a sincere human embrace.
And, although you may encounter the narcissist as having little consideration for your feelings and needs, as someone solely willing to harvest your attention via a self-obsessed sense of entitlement, the simple truth is that the narcissist also desires a heartfelt and much deeper connection. A desire that he cannot comprehend, realise, or accept.

The narcissist is destined to view the idea of an intimate emotional connection as pathetic and inadequate. And as a result of his unrealised yearnings, the narcissist continues to seek your attention via unnerving behaviours. The origins of narcissism

Once upon a time, this self-absorbed peacock was simply a child who had needs, wants and feelings, quite similar to any other child who enters this world.
What reasons led that child to a supposed need to be centre stage, where the rules apply to everyone else but not to him?
In the following section, well dive deep into various plausible explanations and theories that have been put forward by scholars over the years.

**THE SPOILT CHILD**

One theory puts forward that a narcissist possibly grew up in an environment where the assumption of being better than others and possessing exclusive privileges and rights was modelled.
This is usually an environment where decreased limits and lack of consequences were set.
The narcissist's parents most likely failed to teach him how to manage discomfort adequately.
This sort of upbringing shaped his behaviour and set the foundation for the evolution of the spoilt narcissist.

**THE DEPENDENT CHILD**

Another theory is that one parent may have worked tirelessly to enable the child to have as much of a pain-free life as feasibly possible. Instead of aiding and teaching the child to learn skills for undertaking tasks and social interactions, his parents most probably did everything for him.
As a consequence, he learned that he was dependent and helpless instead of discernment of personal competence.

**THE LONELY CHILD**

One of the most accepted theories for the origin of narcissism is that the child was raised in an environment where love was based on achievement.
His parents most likely instilled the idea that being anything short of exceptional meant he was unlovable, flawed, and inadequate.
He may have been influenced to think that love is contingent.
His parents feed their own ego with a sense of pride through his accomplishments, signifying that he was not to embarrass them with an imperfect performance. This type of manipulation led the narcissist to believe he would have his emotional needs met if he endeavoured greatness.

Alternative treatment methods from each parent may have compounded the situation.
In these environments, the child is frequently critiqued by one parent and made to feel like they will never be good enough. However, they may be overprotected by the other parent.
In response to this emotional manipulation and deprivation, the child forms an approach to life with a focus around principles such as; I will look after myself, and nobody is trustworthy.
Unfortunately, the child was not loved for being himself and was neither encouraged to discover his true desires. He was not taught empathy nor how to feel the emotions of another person.
Instead, he was continuously bombarded with shame and criticism, leading the child to believe he was weak for craving attention and a sense of comfort.

**THE MIXED CHILD**

It is also quite possible to find that the narcissist portrays a mixture of the described origins theorised above.

Given the complexity of interactions, it's not surprising that people develop their character traits as a result of a unification of factors.

**SPOILT + DEPENDENT:**

The narcissist in your life could possibly be characterised as having been dependent as well as spoilt.
If this is the case, they may not solely act and feel superior, and may also portray characters traits and signs of incompetence and dependency.
As an adult, the narcissist may develop an entitled attitude, and he may show signs and expect to be doted on.
He may also avoid exercising initiative and making choices due to the fact that he has an underlying fear exposing his own personal shortcomings and failures when undertaking common decisions of life.


**DEPRIVED + DEPENDENT:**

Another combination that possibly might describe your narcissist is both a mixture of a deprived and dependent type.
In this scenario, the narcissist will be offended easily as well as showing signs of dependency, needing continuous external validation and reassurance.
This blend of narcissism can come across as hypersensitive, instead of demanding and ego-centric.
He may show signs of addictive coping mechanisms such as overeating and could most probably be referred to as high maintenance.

Although some scholars hypothesise that the demonstrations of narcissism may expand from biologically pre-determined personality traits, most suggest that they occur due to the succession of the child's early environment and experiences, and biological makeup.

It's interesting to put forth that many children are raised in similar environments to those mentioned above without developing narcissistic behavioural traits.

These children may have encountered an alternative outcome because of a loving family member, teacher, role model who aided in the inculcation of healthy coping mechanisms and tools.

# The Disappearing act

The narcissist is on a continuous quest for excellent emotional autonomy, signifying that he doesn't need anyone and can only truly count on himself.
His personal desires and hardships are usually concealed underneath a camouflage of power, righteousness, success or a combination of all.
He might be the attention seeker, the master of ceremonies, or the contester. Perhaps he is perpetually ready to save the distressed, entertain with witty metaphors or storytelling.
Nevertheless, his emotional incompetence, due mainly to his detachment, is limiting to his capability to empathise or impedes it all together.

Empathy, this perceived sense of the other, is the capacity and the eagerness to envision being in the other person's position. It can be distinguished from sympathy in that it is not solely feeling sadness for another's pain; it is the technique of harmonising with it. It is one of the most intensely connective characteristics of a wholesome relationship, and its deficiency can be disastrous.

*"Daniel Goleman, suggests that someone who doesn't empathise with others can treat them as objects rather than as people."*

**HIDE & SEEK**

The narcissist's shortage of empathy can appear in several ways. For example, if you are eventually able to get a word into a discussion with a narcissist, inviting him to tune in to your world, he's prone to swiftly convert to the wondrous Houdini, vanishing before your eyes. He may actually walk away in the midst of your sentence or declare an extraordinary "something" that he must attend to immediately.

And when life bestows you with an additional critical situation, such as a health difficulty or other personal trauma, the narcissist becomes more firm in his absenteeism. Abruptly you discover yourself necessitating to focus on yourself, perhaps struggling for your life, yet the now "inconvenienced" narcissist becomes even further obnoxious, self-centred, or checked out.

**HIDING BEHIND COPING MECHANISMS**

The narcissist's reactions are sudden and assorted. He may attempt to make you feel stupid and irrational for putting forth a demand or asserting a grievance by belittling your "silly" emotional necessities. He may talk over you with a continuous monologue for vast amounts of time.

He may extend a reply similar to "I don't know what you want from me," then designate all ways in which he is most excellent human of all and above any kind type objection.

Narcissists continuously hide their shortcomings so that no one can use, humiliate or disappoint them again. Nevertheless, skulking behind this deceptive defiance implies they sacrifice many authentic pleasures and griefs and, along with them, many of their core's desires.

If you find yourself in a romantic partnership with a narcissist, he may feel the ominous rise of that lonely child the moment you ask him for some insight into his emotional realm, or even when you encourage him to understand yours better.

This deficiency of emotional affection can leave you encountering feelings of loneliness, even when the narcissist is right by your side.

*Marion Solomon, PhD, puts forth the idea that the narcissist fears the dissolution of a sense of self when entering an emotional relationship. For narcissists, intimacy seems like a stifling and unsafe terrain.*

**THE NARCISSISTS MANTRA**

I will need no one is the reverberating and self-affirming refrain of the narcissist, especially for male narcissists. You owe me is more often than not a female narcissist's recurrent refrain. These underlying thought patterns are entirely outside of the narcissist's consciousness—an involuntary tune that frequently plays in the backdrop thanks to well-established memory loops. This complex memory system is also where self-preserving masks that assist with a variety of coping mechanisms reside.

**THE MASKS**

The narcissist's masks allow him to mould conceivably unpleasant experiences into tolerable, perhaps even pleasant ones. Wearing a mask is a way to slip into another mode of being when confronted with distressing and upsetting feelings. These masks are also more commonly known as a coping mechanism.
Here are some of the most common character altering coping mechanisms of the narcissist:

- The bully
- The show-off

- The addictive self-soother
- The entitled one

## A Narcissist's Strategy

Based on their inherent and explicit memories of unmet childhood necessities, multiple narcissists manifest the ideal that such needs will never be satisfied later on in life.
This fear is at the core of the narcissist's superficial and unanimated attachments to others. He counterbalances the fear of not having his needs met through an extravagantly self-sufficient persona. This blend of overcompensation and fear ultimately leads to a deficiency of intimacy with ones-self.

When a narcissist tries to evade these complicated feelings, he may automatically slip into one of the many coping methods listed earlier, wearing whatever mask best fits his requirements in the given situation.

These maladaptive coping methods create some of the characteristically adverse behaviours you may be undergoing with the narcissist in your life. Regrettably, these masks actually perpetuate the sentiments he attempts to evade, re-creating the humiliation, scepticism, and divestment of his initial experiences.

For example, in an attempt to not feel his discomfiture in a social environment, he will lament being bored or will propel into one of his monologues. Consequentially, he will look not only uncomfortable but arrogant and offensive as well.

*Jeffrey Young, the original founder of schema therapy and an expert in the field of narcissism, writes about the huge detriments of concealing one's true self. He explains how the narcissist may look content on the surface of his fictitious self, but beneath that, he still feels inadequate.*

## Example Of Covert Narcissism

Often, narcissists show up in concealed packaging and proceed to dazzle you with pompous, if subtle, gentry. These morally sanctimonious narcissists are endlessly pointing out the "right" and "wrong" way of living. They are unendingly distinguishing themselves from "intolerant people" and those that are "self-centred and apathetic." These types of clandestine narcissists are keen to find resolutions to all of your predicaments.

The covert narcissist arrogantly claims allegiance to the truth. He extends his indisputable humbleness and human defect in an attempt to sway you. Hiding behind this curtain, he bashfully confesses his commitment to meticulous self- improvement.

He might say, "Sure, I could continue discussing the fifteen-thousand-dollar benefaction I made to the cancer foundation, but I'm not that sort of a person. I don't need approval for my charitable actions."

Like all narcissists, he yearns for acclaimed credit, so it's just a matter of time before he is apprehended by the ongoing torture of the deprived child within, who's only desire is to be acknowledged. He hides that bothersome child back within himself and exposes his hunger and desire for acknowledgement as a remarkable human being. With little to no patience for his simplistic yearnings for love and connection and little trust in the likelihood of attaining them, the narcissist aims for recognition and validation in a quest to assert his prominently disclosed emotional autonomy.

It is especially challenging for him to flee the pain he feels when the recognition being awarded to him for his charitable acts, aren't dramatic enough, or the spotlight dims too soon. In time, bitterness and disappointment about his lack of perpetual praise set in, descending upon whoever appears to be in his way.
You may be treated to a sly criticism on the careless and idiotic nature of bureaucracies.

Because he is disillusioned at enduring less than a five-minute standing ovation for his appearance in the public eye, he counterattacks the understood enemies of his ego with self-righteous displays or punishing critiques, and through this outburst, he winches himself back upon his holier-than-thou throne.

# The Contrast between Male and Female Narcissists

Many characteristics are similar in both male and female narcissists. Both can be distinguished by their love affair with the sound of their own voice and their perpetual search for everlasting appreciation. Both will attack you with their beliefs, grievances, and objections until you become bored to tears. If you attempt to speak while they're giving a monologue, you'll abruptly become non-existent. And because they have yet to acquire the aptitude for empathy, they don't recognise that their attempts to dazzle you, are really drowning you with illusions a quick exit from their suffocating ambush.

Due to the sheer fact that the vast bulk of narcissists are male, the references in this chapter— and throughout the book—tend to concentrate on how narcissism displays in men. However, females make up 20 to 25 % of narcissists, and they usually display distinctive features. So, let's go ahead and examine what differentiates these divas from male narcissists.

**HER MAJESTY**

The female narcissist may be a temptress who entraps you with flirtatious behaviour. An especially prevalent type of female narcissist is the martyr or victim: She might seize you with her victimised speech on how much she has to do, has done and does that she won't be recognised for. This master victim is rarely far away from her succeeding emotive purge. Should you declare that you are ill or that you're running delayed for an interview, your necessities will dissolve within the energy of her vast self-absorption.

She will sense it if you attempt to oppose or overlook her, and she'll make you requite by sulking, crying, or perhaps even warning to leave you or harm herself. Conquered by fear, you may contribute an apology and pledge to tend to her needs in a better manner. You may put forth justifications, claiming you must be exhausted or occupied and weren't thinking coherently. You may even celebrate her for her graciousness and thank her for providing you with another opportunity.

The narcissistic woman will have your innermost core manipulated and running circles around itself. Should you struggle to abide by her impetuous dramatics and retrieve your clear mindedness, she will slowly slip into a spectacle of pouts, and rude smugness.

**FEMALE NARCISSISTIC VANITY**

Narcissistic women usually put more emphasis on their physical presence in comparison to narcissistic men, eagerly displaying their bodily qualities. Female narcissists also place more importance on always wearing a high fashion, and children who are meticulously dressed. In this technologic age, an interpretation for this trend in the importance of status might be down to contentious stereotypical gender socialisation.

Blogger Susan Walsh draws some compelling considerations about this trend:

*"During the 70s and 80s, Americans became obsessed with celebrity culture and eating disorders skyrocketed. Today, social media breeds narcissism by constantly encouraging women to post flattering photos and create online profiles that stress their uniqueness. [Social media sites] require self- promotion, bringing out the narcissist in us. Reality shows promote the most ordinary, unimpressive people as special, and we follow their dysfunctional lives with fascination.... Female narcissists see their lives as a*

*running feature film with them in the lead, receiving accolades at all times."*

The ground for concern is supported by data on narcissism from the research of students and young adults exhibiting a culture of entitlement and self-absorption. Under this self-perpetuated performance, they come to think that the only elements that matter in life are physically looking fabulous, surpassing in accomplishments and performance, obtaining the consideration of relevant people, and placing themselves adequately; and that if they implement these actions, they will achieve everything they could ever desire. They aren't preoccupied about the necessities of others or the consequence of their behaviour on others except if it impedes their self-righteous road to success by getting in the way of what they desire. Furthermore, and with noticeable distinction from the male narcissistic type that often presents itself in the forms of self-doubt and insecure vulnerability, this growing variety of female narcissists is a blend of sentimental sweetness and sophisticated self-entitlement.

# Healthy Narcissism

Narcissism sounds like a tragedy, does it not? But is narcissism invariably a negative thing?
In all honesty, it's not. Wholesome narcissism carries the traits of confidence and pride. Moreover, "salubrious narcissism" seems like an oxymoron, when in fact, narcissism befalls along a spectrum inside the human mind. Integrated with human nature is an inclination for narcissistic interpretation. And that isn't at all negative.

**HEALTHY CHILDHOOD NARCISSISM**

If you examine the research on childhood development, you'll discover that almost every child comes into the world with the ability to be spontaneous, angered, and commanding. These characteristics are simply portions of the broad spectrum of sentiments associated with a child's innate vulnerability and natural character. Narcissism has a sturdy advantage for children. It encourages them to reveal their physical and heartfelt distress, particularly in earlier ages. The child displays anger, laments, and commands attention in order to receive assurance, support, compassion, and security. This is considered wholesome age-appropriate behavioural responses.

A thoughtful and passionate method to parenting attempts to accommodate the emotional and physical assistance that will enable the child to mature securely and proficiently. It strives to contribute to sound boundaries that then aid to promote security and compassion.
It seeks to encourage a healthy equilibrium between the consciousness of others and self-directed awareness. Most parents want their children to mature with knowledgeable and caring values, and a salubrious sense of entitlement, indicating

that they will preserve their sense of self-worth. Parents also desire for their children to obtain sensitivity and reverence for the virtues of others. And they must endeavour to do all of this with their own lingering doubts, and their child's individual personality. This can certainly be a challenging responsibility for any parent.

In a warm and caring parent-child bond, the notion of embarrassment can present a relevant role in the discipline as a method of teaching the child a discernment of values and individual accountability without indicating that the child is defective and bad. With this strategy, the child discovers how to be responsible without feeling damaged and imperfect. The purpose is to construct a home where the child learns to honour her creativity and individuality while also cultivating a sense of accountability to the identity of others.

In essence, healthy childhood narcissism develops into sincerity—the art of composing a promise and conserving it. It facilitates the child to verbalise her intentions, wants, and desires in the world with transparency and delicacy to others. Salubrious narcissism fosters empathy, promoting feelings of accountability and mutuality.

**HEALTHY ADULT NARCISSISM**

When analysing the term "healthy adult narcissism," you may utilise a specific person as a point of reference, someone who has accomplished a measure of popularity or recognition and who is presently making an impact in the community or in society as a whole. This person may also be having a thorough influence on your life. People who display healthy adult narcissism may or may not have been fortuitous enough to experience all the benefits of wise and kind parenting and a steady and wholesome home in which to develop and grow.

Their inceptions may have been dark and intense, and their life course may have taken them through difficult times.

While forms of prosperity and celebrity are oftentimes prominently upheld by repellent people with apparent negative forms of narcissism, many auspicious people populate the realm of healthy, narcissism. Why do we still want to use the expression "narcissism" with this assemblage?
Partly, it's because these people, who regularly possess above-average skill and determination, aren't like the common stereotypical "nice guy" when it comes to self-confidence and their ability toward dealing with adversaries.

So how might we distinguish healthy adult narcissists?
Typically, they hold many of the subsequent traits and expose them frequently and with enthusiasm:

Empathy: They are harmonised to the emotional world of others.
Engaged: They are charismatic, socially intelligent, and interpersonally cordial.
Leader: They can imagine a purpose or a concept and can form a course when co-operating, among others.
Oneself: They are committed to philanthropy and authenticity.
Recognition: They are kindled by positive admiration and prompted to make a difference.
Determination: They can push beyond impenetrable barriers of competition.
Confrontation They hold others answerable, but without slaying their personalities.
Fear: They can differentiate between moderately disturbing solicitation and unfavorable seduction.

# Nature VS nurture

Narcissism has become so generalised that the number of pure guesswork going on does damage to the average person trying to comprehend this disorder.

Is Narcissistic Personality Disorder Genetically Obtained?

Simply because Narcissistic Personality Disorder (NPD) tracks through families does not imply that it is genetically acquired. Narcissistic battery courses through those families also. That's a couple of variables, either or both of which could be liable. Science can't conclude data with more than one variable.

Since narcissists switch up their persona as and when they please, their harmful behaviour is treated as volatile under the law in certain countries.
Furthermore, most narcissists offspring do not end up following in their footsteps and are very rarely considered narcissists.
Therefore, the genetic theory behind narcissism requires much further research before being considered as a plausible cause.
Diseases can often have more than one cause, therefore presumably the conclusion that will be drawn by the scientific community is that specific genetics can create and allow a predisposition for NPD.

Also, it's possible that some genes accountable for hard-wired circuitry in a newborn infant could damage healthy development and therefore cause some cases of NPD.
We see something similar with autism: supposedly, children born blind are much more prone to become autistic and need to be actively raised to help the infant unite with an outside world he cannot perceive. However, blindness is not the typical cause of autism, and we will plausibly find that genetics aren't the common root of NPD.

Nevertheless, we shall have to wait for science to let us know for certain.

## IS IT PROMPTED BY A CHEMICAL IMBALANCE?

The corresponding amounts of particular neurotransmitters are often
linked with psychological difficulties. But that doesn't imply that an imbalance produced the problem. The imbalance may entirely be caused by another more significant difficulty.

For instance, after the passing of someone close to us, we are customarily depressed for a while. The unhappy feelings and thoughts of loss cause the brain cells associated with creating specific neurotransmitters. As the concentration of these neurotransmitters grows, it demands less stimulus to create that uneasy feeling we perceive in grief. Thus, the enhanced level of the "saddening" neurotransmitters makes us conceive further depressed thoughts, freeing more of those neurotransmitters that make us feel pessimistic and so on. This process is referred to as runaway feedback and is easily turned into a vicious cycle.

However, the brain is a phenomenal organ with multiple internal control systems. For instance, raised levels of these "depressing" neurotransmitters also supplies back to decrease the threshold for stimulation in the circuitry that causes us to laugh. In other terms, nature provides us with chemistry that heightens our sense of humour at before-mentioned times. Everything seems more entertaining. Not only throughout moments of depression but during times of shock and notable pressure. This phenomenon is most commonly referred to as the "foxhole humour."

This counterbalancing is an outstanding representation of how the body defends and heals itself. Hence, ordinarily, following our loss, we get back into the routine of life and its distractions. As time passes, our happier feelings and our innate desire to be felicitous gradually induce the concentrations of those "depressing" neurotransmitters to lower back to normal levels again.
Hence why a depression produced by such circumstances is seen as normal except if it endures for prolonged amounts of time. Transient use of medication that rebuilds the balance faster can also be effective.

Although, of course, a person predisposed to depression by constant continued thought patterns or some open-ended situation will soon display depression once again when drug therapy is discontinued.

Hopefully, medications will be discovered that can support narcissists through the discomfort of confronting their true selves in talk therapy. This would make them less opposed to talk therapy and thus give the method an adequate chance to work.

**PSYCHOLOGICAL REASONS**

Many researchers believe that the affliction of malignant narcissism is carried down from generation to generation through narcissistic exploitation of a child.
However, a brief word of warning before jumping to the assumption that parents are to blame.

NPD hasn't been researched nearly as much as it's next-door-neighbour, Antisocial Personality Disorder (psychopathy).
Recent research has brought into question whether they are at all distinct. Of course, only a diminutive subset of all psychopaths have been analysed — principally those in the prison group. But leading researchers in psychopathy say that they seldom come from lovely homes.

Anyone who has been raised in a home with a narcissistic parent understands that, to all visible appearances and as far as anyone knows, it's a pleasant home life. But in reality, it's a living nightmare.
Therefore, researchers could be mistaken psychopaths/narcissists could all be proceeding from abusive upbringings. But not all the children from those environments turn out like their parents.
Hence, there definitely is a component of choice in the affair.

# PART II COMMON MYTHS ABOUT NARCISSISM

**MYTH 1: NARCISSISM IS SIMPLY HIGH SELF-CONFIDENCE**

Narcissism is regularly conceived to be a case of high self-confidence. Narcissists do possess high self-confidence, and in reality, many methods used to enhance self-confidence might drive to higher narcissism. But narcissism and self-confidence differ. Narcissists believe they are more intelligent, exceptionally good looking, and more significant than others, although not significantly more virtuous, caring, or more sympathetic.

Narcissists don't boast about how they are the kindest, most considerate people within society, but they do enjoy stating that they're champions or that they are attractive. People simply high in self-confidence also possess assertive views of themselves, but they also see themselves as caring and trustworthy. Furthermore, this is one of the fundamental reasons narcissists lack objectivity.

For example, if you win a ping-pong match to a close friend, you normally don't yell absurdities such as "Loser". Narcissists are missing the key element of having consideration for others, which is why their arrogance often becomes uncontrollable.

**MYTH 2: NARCISSISTS ARE TIMID AND HAVE LOW SELF-CONFIDENCE**

Many people assume that narcissists are actually shy and riddled with self-loathing. Their self-importance is just a mask for their rooted insecurities regarding themselves. This view can be traced back to some elements of psychodynamic hypothesis, which contemplate that narcissism is a safeguard toward an "abandoned" or "angered" self, burdened with hidden low self-confidence, or a tremendous sense of guilt.

This debate is flawed and puts forth the ideal that we should write off narcissistic personalities as imperfect beings who just need to realise how to love themselves—our society's answer to everything.

We can choose to think that narcissists are hurting even when they seem happy and egotistic. This theory also interlinks with several psychodynamic descriptions of behaviour in which the deliberate and unconscious are opposed.

The "mask toward insecurity" representation of narcissism is pervasive in our society.

On TV's Grey's Anatomy, a coworker braves a mean, bitingly satirical medical resident by stating, "What is it about your want to deprecate other people? Does humiliating someone feed what little self-confidence you're clasping? I can't even commence to envisage what occurred in your life to make you the kind of character that everybody loathes." The customarily confident medical resident seems flustered and quickly releases the papers he's carrying, which is a TV stenotype for "You're accurate. You learned the suppressed truth about my unfortunate worthless soul."

A lot of the accessible news about narcissism is based on the inaccurate doctrine that narcissists have low self-confidence.

An online site states that narcissists "really have low self-confidence and encounter a sense of self-doubt around others. It is this anxious feeling that compels them to extend a theatrical representation of themselves as a whole."

Celebrity life coach Patrick Wanis told MSNBC, "Paris Hilton is suffering from narcissism. Although she appears to be confident, she is, in reality, vulnerable, self-important, and has low self-confidence."

Many people perceive self-doubt as the significant distinction between narcissism and self-assurance; you can feel fabulous by praising yourself, but if you're confident, it's not narcissism.

Nevertheless, there is no proof that the extraverted narcissists we concentrate on in this book have low self-confidence or are troubled underneath—they admire themselves, and even more so than the ordinary person.

Adults who obtain high scores on narcissism usually score high on self-confidence also.

The universal self-confidence test has items like "I consider I am a person of value, at least on an even keel with others" and "I sense that I have several salutary qualities."

To narcissistic people, these self-confidence items appear like a metaphor of their own self-importance. "Of course, I'm a person of value—more so than most people!" they think. "I possess many high-grade qualities, not just simply a number of them!"

Narcissists do have sporadic periods of low self-confidence and can seek treatment, but in this book, we concentrate more on the culturally savvy narcissists, who have the most considerable influence on societal psychology.

Much of the uncertainty about narcissism originates from believing that most narcissists are similar to these defenceless narcissists, but they're not.

Perhaps, deep down inside, they do despise themselves, and their narcissism is a protective camouflage for their shortage of true self-confidence.

New approaches in social psychology have made it much simpler to clarify such enigmas. The Implicit Association Test

(IAT), developed by Tony Greenwald, measures how quickly people can connect two ideals.

The IAT was utilised initially to measure ethnic prejudice.

In that account, photographs of white and black faces appear on a screen alongside words like positive and negative. In the first step, test takers push the key on the side of the console under "positive" if a white face surfaces and under "negative" if a black face emerges. They later do the opposite, matching white faces with "negative" and black faces with "positive." The computer tracks how fast people take to push the key for each pair; being able to match white faces with "positive" quicker than black faces reveals a preference for whites.

Many people who display limited discrimination in specific surveys still show an inherent ethnic prejudice on this quiz. Writer Malcolm Gladwell, who penned about unconscious connections in his book, and who is biracial himself, was flustered to realise that he noticed it arduous to pair black faces with "positive" but straightforward to do the equivalent for white faces. The test is an intriguing measure of our authentic beliefs—the unconscious associations and belief systems we have learned from our society.

Researchers have recently modified the IAT to measure self-confidence, with testers matching keys for "self" and "not-self" with positive and contradictory words. People with large amounts of confidence find it straightforward to connect themselves with positive words like kind and pleasant but respond much slower when attempting to pair "self" with offensive and evil. Some researchers have employed this system to identify how narcissists genuinely feel about themselves.

It turns out that narcissists believe they're amazing.

Narcissistic people found it even more natural than non-narcissists to tap the key for "self" when words such as great, beautiful, amazing, and honest and found it evenly, if not more challenging to push the "self" key for words like regretful, offensive, terrible, and injustice.

Narcissists also had more distinguished unconscious self-confidence than non-narcissists on elements such as confident, enthusiastic, dynamic, frank, powerful, and passionate.
Narcissists obtained average on words like loving, selfless, supportive, friendly, and devoted, but even in this realm, they dispensed no indications of feeble self-image.

An alternative way to look at unconscious self-confidence is with the "name-letter test," in which researchers invite people to rank the letters in the alphabet according to how attractive or agreeable they are — listing the letters in your own name as more likeable or charming is an immeasurable sign of internal self-confidence.
Sure enough, narcissists perceive the letters in their name as powerful and confident. Again, narcissism is not about bottomless self-loathing or low self-confidence, but faith in personal achievement sections matched with a depressed disposition toward affection and emotional intimacy with others.
Considering narcissism as a mask for self-doubt is a significant issue, as many people believe that narcissism can be healed with further amounts of self-admiration. It can't.
Increased self-confidence, particularly if it spans into narcissism, will solely make that predicament worse. Consequently, it is imperative that programs attempting to work with school tyrants be very mindful when attempting to grow their self-confidence, as the development of narcissism might result as a consequence. Bullies need to acquire regard for others.

They already have more than enough reverence for themselves.

**MYTH 3: NARCISSISTS ARE BETTER THAN EVERYONE ELSE**

Perhaps narcissists are warranted in their beliefs that they are exceptional because they really are. It assuredly would be more straightforward to be narcissistic if you were truly beautiful or expressly gifted at something, but there isn't much proof that narcissists are any better.

Two research studies found that narcissists didn't get any higher points on real IQ tests, and another observed no association between narcissism and achievement on a test of overall knowledge.

Research studies on creativity are mixed, with one attaining a positive association and another finding no link.

Narcissists also aren't more attractive: across multiple studies, strangers who rated photographs found narcissists no more beautiful than others, even though they believed they were more good-looking.

Nevertheless, narcissists do know how to pluck out a favourable picture of themselves. For example, the photographs that narcissists chose for their private Websites were deemed as more attractive by viewers. Overall, narcissists think that they are more intelligent and far more appealing than they truly are.

**MYTH 4: A LITTLE NARCISSISM IS HEALTHFUL**

Supposing that loathing yourself is the alternative to admiring yourself is a misleading substitute. Just as obesity scholars are not stating that Westerners should all become anorexic, I am also not implying self-loathing. A modest amount of people do loathe themselves and could use some self-confidence. But you can admire yourself, without relishing yourself to excess.

It would be more useful for everyone not to ponder on self-feelings—good or bad— so much. Alternatively, concentrate on life: your connections with others, your profession, or the excellence of the physical world.

Recall the most immeasurable joy you encountered in life— it doesn't normally come from believing about how fabulous you are. Rather, it comes from uniting with the world and detaching from yourself, such as when you enjoy moments with colleagues, family, and kids, are happy at work, or do meditative activities such as painting, journaling, working out, or supporting others.

Is any volume of narcissism good?
The genuine question is, "Healthful for who?"

Self-indulgence, for example, might enable you to get a more significant piece of cheesecake after dinner but will spoil your longer-term connections with your friends and might lose you a dinner invite in the future.
A narcissist would plausibly be on the principal life-raft on a submerging ship—adaptive, yes, but not warranted if he's robbing a place on the boat from a child.
Harming others is sinful, and that belief familiarises our position on whether self- praise is healthful. Narcissistic behaviour that produces others to suffer isn't "good." Narcissism at the cost of one's own achievement is also not healthful. Feeling a dash of emotion and self-confidence from being a legend in your personal consciousness seems slightly unhealthy, but then again, if it serves you and isn't unfavourably influencing others in your presence, I'm not going to make a huge deal out of it.

Therefore, narcissism that improves achievement but does not harm others, such as the courage and self-admiration you might require before a public appearance, is the somewhat more salubrious viewpoint of narcissism, although there are presumably other methods to get the same outcome without concentrating so much on the self.

**MYTH 5: NARCISSISM IS SIMPLY VANITY**

Although vanity is unquestionably one of the adverse aspects of narcissists, it is not the only one. Narcissists are also greedy, spoilt, offensive when provoked, and detached in emotional intimacy.

# PART III TREATMENT FOR NARCISSISTIC BEHAVIOUR

The following ideals are drawn from the works of Daniel Siegel, Aaron Beck, and Jeffrey Young can serve to elucidate the way you cope with the narcissist in your life.

In this chapter, I'll utilise the acumens of these authorities to take a solid look at the idea of life themes and the influence of natural impulses. While the weight is still focused on comprehending the narcissist, I'll also prompt you to reflect on your own accounts and notice how the mould of the mind and the biology of the brain can bestow fearsome difficulties. This knowledge will help you recognise what is needed for growth and transformation in your relationship with a narcissist.

# Cognitive Therapy

Aaron Beck, known more commonly as the father of cognitive therapy, has given innumerable therapists and self-help readers a helpful compass for operating the complicated terrain of our emotional and mental belief systems.

His investigation and clinical applicability of cognitive therapy are globally recognised, and his strategy has regularly been demonstrated profoundly effective in aiding people to modify and develop dysfunctional patterns of thought and behaviour.

For example, as the narcissist learns to explore and carefully re-write his rhetoric of the world, along with all of its biased hypotheses, he is released from the deeply-rooted patterns of behaviour that point to his troublesome coping mechanisms, which you end up suffering when in his proximity.

Cognitive therapy permits for an exploration of the definitions we assign to the people, locations, and material things in our lives. It presents, through a mixture of theories and approaches, a means for adjusting the biased presumptions that are often linked to our adverse emotional experiences and victimising patterns of behaviour.

When presented in reference to narcissism; cognitive therapists promote a collaborative method by which the narcissist generates a more authentic collection of opinions, and ideals, replacing the warped thoughts that have remained rooted in his mind in respect to self, society, and the future. The importance is placed on generating a mindful awareness to self-talk and questioning the reality of often biased personal dialogues. This form of work has produced the foundations for the increase of other types of therapy, especially schema therapy, which has its origins in Beck's method.

# Schema Therapy

Jeffrey Young is the creator and founder of schema therapy, an integrative type of psychotherapy merging proven cognitive and behavioural methods with other broadly exercised therapies, such as interpersonal, and gestalt therapy. He has made this method available to the general public in books such as Reinventing Your Life and has further increased the reach of this potent form of therapy through books for specialists, such as Schema Therapy: A Practitioner's Guide.
Recent examinations show that schema therapy grants extraordinary results when applied with complex clients, and it is a considered a preferred and powerful treatment plan for dealing with matters of narcissism.

**UNDERSTANDING SCHEMAS**

Young's schema therapy suggests eighteen early maladaptive schemas that arise in adulthood as dysfunctional life themes. They are also attributed to as "life traps."
They are viewed as early maladaptive schemas because they're originated from troubling childhood and adolescent occurrences where primary needs are not satisfactorily met, which conflicts with healthy and durable growth.

Schemas are comprised of ideals or cognitions. They also include bodily and emotional sensations, along with biological components such as temperament.

Temperament points to the inherent characteristics of the child. Along with attitude, motor skills, and capabilities for concentration, each child displays certain natural preferences, such as nervousness, aggressiveness, introspection, sympathy, adjustability, resilience, and so on. These natural preferences are formed by genetic makeup, and they are exposed and visible in the early stages of a child's development.

For example, when faced with new experiences or strangers, some young children express an avoidant trend and clasp to their parent or a familiar article.
Because environmental impacts can develop and transform the natural capabilities of a child, character arises from the interaction of the child's personality and the environment.

For instance, if a bashful child is continually rejected and embarrassed by a parent, she might form a heightened inclination to withdraw. Paradoxically, such a child might counter with both hostile acts of disagreement or submissive avoidance and detachment. A child in this environment could conceivably develop an adverse self-appraisal, also referred to as a defectiveness schema.

On the other hand, if a parent dispenses tolerance and acceptance in respect to the child's distress and shyness, leading her ever so kindly to take modest steps beyond her comfort zone, this could possibly help the child master a sense of self-confidence in several new and social circumstances. In this case, self-acceptance displays potentiality.

It is also accurate that temperament can alter as we go through life. It isn't entirely clear what foretells lifelong versus temporary temperament. But we do comprehend that schemas are created as a consequence of the interplay among a child's temperament and the challenges she faces in her environment.

Schemas may be latent for much of one's life, only becoming initiated by distinct situations that either simulate or test the unyielding beliefs integrated within them. Long confined within the mind and exhibiting some of the actualities of the person's childhood, these "revelations" become hard to deny. They are oftentimes attached to painful childhood memories, discreetly concealed within the brain, and are endured as visceral, indicating that they are sensed. Because they arise outside of consciousness and consequently aren't based on the present, the intense and often distorted resonance of schemas commonly drives to self-defeating behavioural patterns.

When schemas are initiated, the effects are comparable to the triggering of traumatic remembrances. The physical and emotional circuits of the brain and body frequently disengage from the decision-making regions of the brain, which are accountable for differentiating between experiences in the present versus those in the past. When schemas are triggered, the resulting discharge of stress hormones short-circuits the supervisory areas of the brain, which ordinarily allow for efficiency in rationalising and logic. If you're working from an absolute state of "there and then," your reactions and judgment making can be impacted by circumstances and sentiments of the past, rather than by what's occurring in the present. Furthermore, you don't even recognise it because it occurs on a subconscious level, outside of your awareness.

For example, if you formed a schema of abandonment due to the unpleasant memory of your father's disappearance when you were five years old, you may be unusually susceptible to the notion of people leaving you. When your husband informs you that he will be travelling for work, you begin to feel that anxiousness and progress to make exorbitant requests for communication and reassurance. This sets the foundation for a relationship filled with issues of doubt and distrust.

We all have schemas, and normally more than one. They are produced in reply to flawed and seldom traumatic early life occurrences. In numerous cases, harmful events such as maltreatment, negligence, abandonment, or extreme control generate schemas that become bound to a child's emotional makeup. This, in unification with biological predisposition, or character, eventually forms the child's personality.

**USING SCHEMAS TO SURMISE INTERPLAYS WITH A NARCISSIST**

You might discover that you and the narcissist in your life have, have matching schemas, which may have arisen from either alike or very distinctive backgrounds.

What distinguishes the two of you, notwithstanding those conceivably comparable schemas, is how you cope with them.

Let's say, for example, that a very generous mom raised you—not merely just generous, but indeed with little ability to communicate her own necessities and desires. She may have been the type of person who evaded disputes and felt uncomfortable when she was the centre of attention. She may have infrequently exhibited symptoms of irritation when she was exhausted and overburdened by her pressure or if she felt suffocated about something vital to her. You may have fostered this schema as a result of observing her actions with people, including the unruly ones. As a consequence, you may activate your self-effacing and subjugation schemas by allowing submission when in reference to the narcissist in your life.

This type of reaction is especially indicative of women.

Regrettably, this coping mechanism will preserve the very schemas you endeavour to escape. The more you give in to your liberal and subjugation ideals; perhaps by allowing the narcissist's poor habits, or by not asserting your opinions as demanded, the more these beliefs will increase ultimately restraining you from growth. It's an unconscious process that, without knowledge, comprehension, and commitment, will continuously arise.

**FOUNDATIONS OF THE NARCISSIST'S SCHEMAS**

Schemas connected with the narcissist usually arise in a situation like the one put forth in the example mentioned below.

Example: Imagine a child who was raised in a home where he was routinely scrutinised and depreciated—where he was compelled to feel undeserving of love and consideration, and where he sequentially formed a defectiveness schema. He also incurred the emotional deprivation schema because his parents didn't give him much kindness, comprehension, or security. His distrust and subjugation schemas were obtained from feeling dominated and lied to by parents who required him to take care of their self-confidence by adhering to their measures for achievement and abandoning his own distinctive adolescence needs. With no meaningful adult to compensate this environment and no improvement self-work done by his demanding, judgmental parents, he grew up with a propensity of solitude and humiliation, along with a deep-rooted feeling that no one would ever suffice his emotional necessities and that he was unlovable and defective.

During childhood, the recurrent and unpleasant feelings associated with these occurrences soon became folders within his brain.
His schemas served as a diagram for his emotional structure. By early adulthood, the mere act of accessing a room full of strangers becomes a schema activating event; he pulls open the folder and, based on the data within, forecasts being judged, overlooked, or discarded by others.

As a child, he endeavoured to escape the pain linked with his surroundings, ascertaining coping mechanisms that incapacitated healthy interpersonal connections but allowed him to flourish among the voids. Those coping mechanisms oftentimes require wearing three protective masks:

- The perfectionist.
- The avenging bully.
- The competitive peacock.

**LEVERAGE AND INCENTIVE**

*Leverage comes in many forms: for example, a possible or genuine meaningful loss, a disabling medical ailment, end of a job, economic uncertainty, legal trials, or seldom the unstoppable pain of isolation or sadness. With leverage, the opportunity for transformation appears.*
*Incentive also assists, though it isn't as straightforward to promote.*
*To the narcissist, the probability of obtaining humiliation-free and guarded relationships, a feeling of belonging, and freedom from the weight of having to demonstrate his self-worth continually, sounds great. But because he has no previous encounter to draw upon and lots of prosperity in the world of extravagant autonomy, these desires are likely to appear unattainable and even impossible.*

# Foundations of Security: Biology and Attachment

Daniel Siegel, a child psychiatrist and expert in relationship dynamics, as well as an authority figure in the evolution of interpersonal neurobiology, suggests that childhood attachment occurrences undeviatingly influence emotions, autobiographical memory, and one's private account. Although Siegel's focal point isn't on narcissists, but his hypotheses casts a considerable amount of enlightenment on this temperament type.

**HABITUAL CREATURES**

As part of the human predisposition, we are primarily guided by memories, both implicit and explicit. This theory confirms the ideas that Jeffrey Young suggests in schema theory and enables us to examine where life themes dwell within the brain—in implicit or explicit memory.

As it turns out, our schemas, or individual life themes, often wind up in the implicit filling cabinet, outside of our consciousness. When they're activated, we may become aware of emotional, bodily, and cognitive alterations without having a clear comprehension of the memories that provoked those changes, and perhaps without even assuming that memories are accountable for those variances. This leads us to feel impotent, lighting the mechanics of transferring from threat to safety

Residing in an activated state is like living in a situation where neural reenactments of an early experiences cloud the current moment.
When sensing a risk or threat, we generally turn to common strategies to rid our demons, quiet the soul, and recast our

appearance to society. Within the filing cabinet of your brain, you have many old outfits to fit your states of mind and disguise your suffering. When compromised, some of us shift into spiteful rivals, some into sanctimonious preachers, and additionally others into dubious perfectionists.

## CONCLUSION

In union with biological makeup, the early experiences can dramatically mould our ideals, feelings, and responses we put forth to the world. Given that we are beings of habit who drift toward the known, it makes sense that early maladaptive schemas can act like a boomerang, often driving us back to where we began notwithstanding our attempts to shift away from that point.

Understanding the intricate mechanisms of the brain presents us with an admiration for change, while also asserting that transformation is conceivable.

For most of us, understanding and affirming the anatomical facts of memory and its associational trends can support to mediate impediments to change, like regret and humiliation.

If the narcissist in your life is agreeable to seeking licensed help, look for a therapist who can be confrontational yet in an empathetic manner.
In a restricted but compelling way, the therapist must reparent the injured side of the narcissist.

If you decide to solicit licensed support for yourself, the therapist should be able to accompany you to an unearthing of your own schemas and personal impediments to healthy assertiveness. This way, your true self can arise with newfound, understanding, empathy, and self-advocacy, and the narcissist can become perceptive, and accountable. This approach heightens the chance of healing the damage and engaging the isolated and valuable ostracised parts of both parties.

In this section, you've read about the numerous types of narcissism, the most common and suffocating being overt maladaptive narcissism. You've read about the roots of narcissism and the consequences of being around narcissists. You've seen cases of how narcissism exhibits and how it might alter by gender. You've also snatched a look at the suggestions for change and transmutation. As you'll see in future chapters, transformation is plausible, but it demands an intrepid execution. Moreover, there is a sense of quietness that takes place among the narcissist and his true self, and you and your most genuine feelings when you're in his company. This isn't unexpected, given the often undesirable and foreseen consequences of real interactions between both of you.

# PART V HEALING AND RECOVERY

Within the context of "sincere" connections, we are given the opportunity to accomplish mental and emotional changes leading to new self-worth, and interactions with others. These connections allow us to form new habits and free ourselves from automatic reflexes linked to the past. Therefore, the aim is to create this sort of connection in your lives with the narcissist, whether that person is a boss, coworker, member of the family, neighbour, companion, life partner, or lover.

Sadly, these last two are generally the most reluctant to change, given the enormity of the relationship's value and how heartfelt your schemes might be for you both.

However, by developing a more "sincere" connection, you open the door to repair your sense of self and the chance of using your collection of abilities to enhance and change your relationship with the narcissist or, if it is absurd, limiting or even ending the relationship.

The following chapters will assist you in sharpening your consciousness, harnessing your courage, and retaining your passion while developing the abilities you need to deal with the narcissist in your life.

# The Effects Of Narcissistic Behaviour

Commonly, when grown-ups realise that a parent who inconveniences them is a threatening narcissist, they respond to finding that the connection was never a mutually symbiotic relationship, but rather a disguised parasitic one. Their words express a powerful sense of disappointment. And they commence finding relief in the understanding that it wasn't their fault, that their parent was not right. In their words, it's a given that they will break this hostile and predatory relationship that is so terrible and hurtful to them.

Keep in mind that NPD is a comprehensive thinking and behavioural framework. If this man is a harmful narcissist, he does the same thing in a thousand ways — every way under the sun at each chance. If his spouse is likely to call him on this insult, he gives it subtly, both to safeguard deniability and to put a more impressive divider between them than the newspaper.

Why? Because if she got a little attention from him by telling him to put down that paper and respond to her, it would destroy him. A true malignant narcissist does not enter the room until the food is served and leaves it the moment he finishes eating. Furthermore, remember that malignant narcissists are unreasonable.

However, if this man were normal and she was complaining that he's making her feel bad, he's going to soften slowly. But if he's a narcissist, he will go the other way, by being cruel; He'll go straight for the jugular and then add even more insult to injury.

Finally, remember that malignant narcissists see everything as objects, so they have no human relationship with anyone, even their own kids. Ordinary people can't imagine harming their own children's self-esteem.

## CO-DEPENDANCE

Common knowledge says that many people have asked 'Must I leave him?' Since they're "co-dependent" or "inverted narcissists,". That is simply a fancy way for saying they're punishment gluttons, that they're getting some small form of enjoyment from being scolded. This is often referred to as the "martyr complex" exists.

But be careful, the victim is usually blamed in these kinds of instances. Furthermore, with healthy scepticism, any excuse that blames the victim should be studied.

Why? Because it is anti-logical.

Remember that society used to blame the victim for sexual assault, racism, and abuse of any other kind. Different forms of blaming the victim go in and out of fashion, but it is as ancient as the Bible to blame the victim (illness or misfortune was punishment for sin), and it goes on forever. It begins in kindergarten and continues in the workplace. Every time the big guy hits a little one, everyone agrees that the little guy has been "asking" for it.

No one ever asks, "Why would he do that?" Because they willingly think the little guy is so feeble-minded or insane, and that he provoked the situation.

Narcissists aren't always incredibly smart. However, they are especially experienced, in light of the fact that they have been playing this game since childhood. So they're devilish.

Consequently, unless a narcissist is manifestly brilliant, he is bound to be underestimated and thought unsuitable for cunning and duplicity. It is stunning how little doubt he stirs as he goes through extraordinary lengths weaving a web that traps a mate by isolating her from others and making her dependent on him financially, socially and emotionally.

## THE CYCLE OF ABUSE

As odd as it sounds, many perfectly normal people get caught in the cycle of abuse. We see it all too often in the Stockholm Syndrome, named after an event, where hostages took their captors' side and clung to them! Since the Middle Ages, inquisitors and torturers have known and benefited from this strange phenomenon and the hapless victims at their mercy. The famous technique of breaking people by the KGB intentionally led to the establishment of mind control.

Experiencing any form of violence is not natural to a person. We are prompted by our instincts "fight-or-flight".

But society blocks this common feeling in our genes by indoctrinating alternate ideologies— the simple-minded notion that divorce or fighting back is wrong. Especially when the abuser dramatises and acts as if they were the victim. Of course, he is hurting: he doesn't want to lose his punching bag!

And so, the cycle of abuse continues to roll. Over her most precious possession, her concept of herself as a good person.
But remember that mental illness is not a character illness. In reality, we are wounded by both people and society, and a large majority of people experience from some mental malady at some point in their life.

Generally, the individuals who don't exacerbate the situation by mishandling their minds with lies, live ordinary lives. Most get over it or handle it all alone. And those who seek counselling are greatly helped to think clearly again.
It's as simple as understanding that we as a society don't blame veterans for having suffered post-traumatic stress. Therefore, we shouldn't place blame on the abused for reducing to a victimhood state.

## DENIAL

Most individuals with a malignant narcissist ultimately decide to break away.
This often requires a lengthy amount of time, but that's no justification for saying that they're gluttons for punishment. A sensualist for punishment never breaks away. So we have to be cautious not to judge too fast. Denial is a powerful thing, and in traumatic circumstances, it becomes instinctive.

Denial is a slippery slope. That's because every time you managed to form a thought that acknowledged reality, you rapidly suppressed it in denial, to stay in the dark. A fine metaphor is; You didn't get out of the situation until the plane was sat on the runway for so long that you began to believe there were terrorists in the cockpit and negotiations were going on. The silent tension so impenetrable that with a knife you could cut it, and everybody would confute. (You were scared to move or speak because you were scared everyone would denounce you, and rip you to pieces with their bare hands, assuming you were a terrorist.) Then, all of a sudden, a young girl in the seat behind you jumped out of fear and was embraced and comforted by two passengers.

So, be careful about denial. It's a dangerous state of mind. The shock tactics and manipulation tactics of a narcissist push you into it. But do not allow yourself to venture there. People don't think clearly when in a state of denial. They believe and act in the most inexplicable ways because they are constrained 180 degrees in the wrong direction by denial.
You wouldn't have boarded that plane if it hadn't of been for denial.

## Four Stages of Transformation

You may discover journaling a valuable addition to this procedure — and generally beneficial. Writing in a journal can be a very pleasant activity. It can also assist you in finding a fresh perspective on dysfunctional relationships and providing a place to start expressing your genuine voice, rehearsing for relationships in the real world.

It can assist with differentiation regarding the four-stage procedure mentioned here, allowing you to see the partial ideas and feelings flooding your brain as they appear on the page before you.

A four-stage situation might look like this:

Observation: You understand that your connection with the narcissist is one in which you give the most, and he does most of the getting— particularly getting his own way. Though you're inclined to feel regretful and apologise for your limitations, he is more likely to make excuses and blame others for his poor behaviour.

Assessment: You can see how the absence of balance in the relationship and your feeling of injustice are related to anxiety and desperation. These emotions have a familiar resonance that is linked to some of your life story's earliest chapters.

Identification: With your new comprehension of early maladaptive schemes, you can see how the culprits behind these weighted emotions are emotional deprivation, defectiveness, self-sacrifice and subjugation schemes.

You can now see that as a kid the narcissist did not receive a sufficient amount of assistance and mental nurturing and that this child generally had a feeling of failing to be sufficient, construct a sturdy fortress out of doing and giving.

This helped you numb the throbbing ache of longing for love and endorsement — a longing you perceived as shameful. On the off chance that you happen to know the narcissist's childhood history, or maybe by utilising what you've gathered from this book, you can also link the dots to name his schemas and start to see patterns in the choreography of his undesirable moves.

Differentiation: The art of understanding the distinction between what was and what is, differentiation enables you to be in your mind and your body progressively—in the present time and place.

Armed with the knowledge that associates blueprints and coping patterns in the dynamics of your relationship, you can set your word weaponry. You acknowledge that you are never again a weak, but rather an adult capable of standing without hiding, blaming, or caving in.

## Boundaries

It is standard advice, similar guidance any expert gives;
Control your boundaries. Protect your personal boundaries, in other words. Make others respect them. (Respect the boundaries of others as well, of course.)
Why? In such a case that you don't, you will cease to exist as an individual. The narcissist (or psychopath) will bust through them to own you, to make you a killer of his will rather than your own, controlling you against yourself like a puppet, without even you knowing it.

Boundaries imprint out your territory. Control of your boundaries is control of your territory, and control of your territory is ownership of it. On the off chance that you let somebody enter your boundaries — that is, if you let him simply make himself at home on your turf as if he owns it — he deals with your psyche. Indeed, infiltrating limits is the art of brainwashing and mind control. Someone penetrates your personal boundaries, the deeper and more frequently, the more control they get.

This is an intense issue when the controller is a narcissist. That's how, as one narcissist I know puts it, he "gets into your head". That is the means by which he makes you believe it's your fault. That's how he makes you feel accountable in abusing you for his behaviour. That's how he traps you in the Cycle of Abuse, so you keep coming back for more.

Therefore, in case you're on a remorseful fit regarding why you continue cherishing that person, why you keep coming back for more, get off. Boundaries busting strategies work on hard troops and CIA agents. So, you've nothing to be embarrassed about. Nothing's wrong with you. You don't like to suffer subconsciously.

**WHAT ARE PERSONAL BOUNDARIES?**

This is an abstract concept that is difficult to describe, but it does not need to be explained to anyone whose boundaries haven't been eaten away. That's because we instinctively understand where our personal boundaries are and when anyone attempts to break them, we feel it. Our instincts lead us to endure the imposition. The only issue is that some individuals are conditioned to ignore their instincts.
Another thing that blurs and weakens boundaries is their prevalent violations that seem harmless and are strongly rooted in custom. They are the standard in the public eye, everyday events that almost everyone considers acceptable and even upright by nearly everybody. Religion's impositions are not the only example. However, they are a phenomenal one due to their depth and scope. Consider religious dietary laws that

choose for you what and when and the amount you may eat. Rules of ritual purity that determine what you can touch. Religious dress codes. Also giving an organisation a chance to choose what you may peruse and think.

## Strategies and Control

**CHARMED AND DISARMED**

As you may recollect, the narcissist has the unremitting ability to exhilarate your senses with his characteristic of charm and beguiling humour. He can make you feel like you're the favoured one, that you must be truly unique to have amassed his attention. And just as you start to swell under his spell, you find yourself searching in the dark for the farewell sign. He will get you the most desirable seat in the house for his swaggering production. In repayment, you're expected to maintain the spotlight unwaveringly upon him, respond affirmatively during his discourses, laugh, never seem to be uninterested, applaud vociferously and regularly, and never, ever assume to accompany him on the stage.

**BAIT AND SWITCH TACTICS**

The narcissist's enchantment is an enticing bait. It's also a powerful tool, as it may prevent you from questioning the possible costs of the bond until you're hooked. Let's take a look at some distinct instances of the clever but typical bait and switch tactics narcissists use. This might assist you in gaining a more transparent viewpoint on the dynamic in your relationship with a narcissist.

**THE VANISHING ACT**

After promising you his continuous attention, the narcissist becomes unavailable. With no guarantee or repentance, he blames you of being self-centred and needy when you feel disconcerted about it.

**THE SETUP**
Having requested your opinions and input with appearing enthusiasm, the narcissist progresses to assassinate your reply and destroy your self-esteem with demeaning critiques.

**JEKYLL AND HYDE.**
Embracing the chance to be your hero, the narcissist will be generously protective when others are mean to you. But he will have no hesitation about casting you to one side with his rude and egotistic tones if you dare to interrupt him or challenge his beliefs.

**INSULT TO INJURY**
The narcissist will show up surprisingly with a big box full of flowers, making you feel inclined to forgive his behaviour. You answer with acts of affection and gratitude, but, conclusively, nothing is ever quite enough for his insatiability, leaving you pulling your hair out between guilt and exasperation. Ultimately, yet again, it's all about him.

**DEVIL'S ADVOCATE.**
Like the chairman of a debate club or a judge in a courtroom, the narcissist welcomes you into a conversation that rapidly becomes either a long-drawn-out monologue, disputatious or highly antagonistic. No matter what your reply—overlooking him, arguing back, begging, or even giving in—he is indifferent.

Do any of these tactics seem familiar? Remember, the narcissist preserves elevated, merciless standards for himself, and for those who encompass his heavenly magnificence. As you have also determined, narcissists have a remarkably high want for acknowledgement, admiration, authority, achievement, and acceptance. They have these necessities because of a fierce internal shame, emotional solitude, and distrust. Sanctimonious behaviour is simply a mask for their emotional turmoil.

Narcissists, as you have also learned, have an exceptionally strong need for their extraordinary recognition, approval, control, victory, and appreciation. They have these necessities as a result of a furious internal current of disgrace, emotional isolation, and mistrust. Self-righteous behaviour is simply a mask.

## Typical Emotional Responses

The narcissist clearly does not feel bound to play according to the same guidelines as the rest of us. These bait and switch manoeuvres are unreasonable and fake, and worse, the personality of the narcissist does not allow an opportunity to challenge the behaviour or negotiate a solution that frustrates the situation.

Each manoeuvre tends to elicit a particular reaction in the lack of fair communication and negotiation.

Insecurity: When the narcissist performs his vanishing act, the uncertainty of his mood and the untrustworthiness of his presence may leave you feeling alone and insecure. This feeling sometimes harks back to memories of unstable relationships during your childhood.

Intimidation: The setup manoeuvre can be quite intimidating, like being softly coaxed to dip your toe into the water just for a piranha to bite it. This manoeuvre can often imitate childhood situations, for example, your parent urging you to pick something from a menu and afterwards condemning you for the decision you made.

Consequently, you figured out how to find some hidden meaning to locate the "right" answer, regardless of whether it wasn't really your own.

Resentment: When the narcissist changes from Dr Jekyll into the odious Mr Hyde, you become angry of his superiority, self-centredness, and inability to compromise, especially if he heroically defended you only fifteen minutes ago. All of a sudden, his support and heroic endeavours do not feel like they are at all about you.

This may feel like those rare moments when your mother's calling you out of your room and inviting you to join her at the table where she had friends. It was good to feel included and wanted, yet within minutes you understood this was only a ploy so she could lounge in everybody's oohs and aahs over what an excellent activity she'd accomplished with you. Once again, you were left obediently holding the focus on her "mom of the year" act.

Provocation: How does the narcissist figure out how to be so delightful when while at the same time adding insult to injury? And why do you always fall for it? It's not because you're stupid, but because you feel great about being cared for and having moments when you're kindly treated. You put it all out there to be energetic about the narcissist's heroism, just to find out that the charming prince you kissed is a frog. You feel provoked by his miniature moments of magic, once again being caught and compelled to pay the cost with another predictable case of warts.

This may be reminiscent of a dynamic with your parents; maybe you savoured your mother's all-too-rare loving attention when you were sick, just to be guilty because she lost sleep while taking care for you.

Powerlessness: The advocate manoeuvre of the devil is mainly a way to elevate the uniqueness of anything about which the narcissist orates, leaving you feeling weary and helpless. You feel like it's a hopeless scenario; in the event that you don't surrender, he'll keep you up throughout the night, coming to his meaningful conclusion and enjoying his own voice's sound.
This can sometimes feel like the powerlessness of being a child, particularly if you've learned to subjugate your voice to a parent or caregiver who wanted you to maintain your thoughts and views to yourself and respect her sacrosanct point of perspective.

You are inherently prepared to defend yourself in all these situations, but you end up feeling provoked, insecure, harassed, fearful, or helpless — ironically, quite unprotected. Why? We have to re-examine how the brain functions to perceive this. When faced with a grizzly bear, your survival mechanisms are restricted. You can attempt to run out of the bear, attempt to battle it, or you can just sit there, frozen in fear, unable to move in any direction.
—Typical reactions to battle, fight or flight. These survival mechanisms are referred to as counterattack, avoidance, and surrender in schema therapy. The reaction often relies on the nature of the risk to some people. For others, it may always seem the same reaction to any threat.

# PART V TIPS AND TRICKS THAT AID RECOVERY

## Mindfulness

In your well-detailed attention with this book thus far, you've dedicated time and effort to creating sense out of your lifestyles, examining your various life issues, and having a full grasp of how your past experience contributes to your luminous and sometimes dusky character.

You've investigated the links among your reports, dispositions, and schemas. You have an experience of why handling a narcissist is specifically difficult for you, in addition to why you might be overwhelmed and attracted to these people. You can specifically and precisely count and understand how you may be triggered and geared up with a new set of skills for having complete knowledge of yourself and the narcissist, and for beginning to speak more effectively and authentically.

The subsequent step is to encapsulate yourself inside the moment fully. Are familiar with the expression "in one ear and out the other." This expression is an extremely good instance of the power of the Teflon-lined brain. Sometimes, things just seem to slide fully out of consciousness.

This freedom can sometimes be unmatched, allowing us to forgo dissonant orchestrations of the mind and memory within the moment. So, when Mr Knows-It-All-and-Does-No-Wrong gets in your face with yet another one of his unthoughtful contributions concerning personal trouble in your lifestyles or goes off on another tangent about how super he is (poorly disguised by way of sophomoric modesty), you get right of entry to the Teflon-lined issue of your brain.

You press your internal "mute" button, power off your schemas, and take a complete, exasperated breath.

Where your "noisy" thoughts previously could have had you feeling flustered, enraged, full of self-doubt, or helpless, your misery now slides away, like raindrops on a car window.

**LIBERATION FROM YOUR MECHANICAL HABITS**

A fully felt experience of who you are and how you came to be your-self, remains an active tool that has shown to achieve successful results.
However, to maximise the efficacy of this tool, you'll need to improve a few supporting skills. The greatest amongst them is the capacity to notice your own dangerous conduct and stop yourself in the act of intentionally continuing with those unhealthy habits.
This is the inception of opening the door to new methods of responding to and interacting with the narcissist in your life.

As part of the human circumstance, you're predisposed to respond and react in a familiar manner and innate recurring behaviours. And while a number of those habits are adaptive and healthy, others hold you hostage within the prison walls of emotionally and physically painful schemas. Therefore, it's far vital to have a clear intellectual overview, along with a truly felt sensibility, of your inner life—specifically the susceptible parts of yourself. A sense of compassion for yourself is likewise essential. This will help you shift your direction and responses amid experience or vulnerability.

Instead of trying to deal with the same antique messages of I'm unlovable, No one could ever meet my needs, I have no rights, It's my obligation to make other humans jovial, etc, you can redirect your attention to greater practical tests, freeing your mind and body from the misery related to these long-held and biased subject matters.

Once you've deconstructed and revised these adverse thought patterns, you have to preserve your new, more equitable truth to commence pushing back your schemas and the things that trigger them, most especially, narcissistic humans.

You now know how to think about being effective within the remits of your mind. And as long as you've got things to reminiscence about, you'll have schemas to control. However, if your loving internal and newly crafted wise voice is a reasonable and attentive intercessor, experiencing far fewer triggering moments is inevitable, and if you are prompted, your past memories could be much less extreme, enabling you to rebuild and recover.

At times, you may slip back into old conduct and discover yourself yet again inhabiting your acquainted prison cell, annoying to be heard, burying your head in your pillow, or numbly observing the walls around you. However, bear in mind, it's simply a slip, not an illustration that you're inherently fallacious or doomed for failure. By utilising this perspective, you'll quickly find that you can hoist yourself up and out of those old thought patterns and schemas, thus returning to the present moment.

Let's take a look at an example.
Say you're at a social occasion and come across Mr Life-of-the-Party-Can't-Even-Remember-Your Name. You slip into your previously intimidated and traumatic mode of having nothing to contribute. This is your cue.
Recognise the familiarity of this sensation and its incoherent beliefs. Take some moments to direct a kind and soothing consciousness toward your inner world, perhaps with a mild,

discreet stretch or a few soft breaths. Remember that your rights and contributions are well preserved, and you're entitled to have a good time without having to pander to the ego of Mr Obnoxious.

Having taken care of your unseen thoughts, you can accurately manoeuvre yourself to restrict your encounters with the narcissist, and when in his presence, you can keep your voice and your integrity.

"Joe is the cheeseburger that I actually need. If he could welcome me into his inner circle, then, I would be able to have a feel of that special experience. However, I recognise that what I really need, and in reality, revel in, is the chokehold—due to the fact I'm already special, and the manner of taking proper care of myself is by having an open arm to welcome healthy human relationship into my life. My mother didn't recognise how to take care of me and make me feel loved and unique for being me. I craved Joe's need to gain my attention, as I feel less inferior because my schema makes me feel as such, that I need to be of high-quality and mingle with the trendy and famous guys so I can really be of relevance. Joe is an elixir for the pain of my sparked feelings. But the reality is, Joe and I have nothing in common, so the only thing he could ever be is a prop in my life. I don't need props. I need friends."

**THE POWER OF MINDFUL AWARENESS**

To see yourself as genuinely like the above Joe example and avoid being trapped by your schemas and falling into old behavioural patterns, it's crucial to expand mindful consciousness.

We've briefly brushed over the subject matter in some of the previous chapters, however now, we'll focus on further growing this skill.

Simply put, mindful attention means paying interest or being attuned in your past memories and sensations, internal and external experience inclusive. You deliberately initiate your sensory system and factor your attention anywhere you choose.

"Being conscious means being privy to everything and certain of nothing."

I love this quote, due to the true fact that as soon as reality enters the arena, the possibilities become eclipsed. The opportunity of seeing and feeling through an entirely new sensory lens is the harvest of the flexible mind. With focus and versatility, you enlist the possibility of seeing with plentiful clarity and become conscious of the field inside or around you.

For example, think of the ocean. With conscious attention, you can hear the sound of the waves more intensely. The sensations heightened with the help of the warm mist and the radiant sun. You can smell and even feel the salty tang in the air.

Being absolutely attuned to your senses allows you to be engaged in a multifaceted experience of the present moment.

**THE IMPORTANCE OF PRACTICE**

Developing a mindfully readjusted brain calls for seasonal practice.
As with anything you choose to learn, repetition and mindset are essential. Think about riding a motorbike or riding a car. Before you were able to take in the scenery, you needed to focus carefully on the positions of your fingers and feet, your posture, steering, speed, and visible cues.

Many years ago, a friend agreed to teach me how to drive a stick shift.

He directed me to a street with a very steep incline during rush hour traffic. He told me that I had to tackle the difficult situations right from the start.

Being an experienced driver of eight years, I felt my sweaty palms clenching to the wheel, my lower back stiff against the seat, and my eyes darting to the rearview side windows, noting the too-comfortable closeness of the vehicle behind me.

Developing this new talent entails severe attention and effort. Yet only a brief time later I found myself driving my newly purchased stick-shift vehicle uphill in traffic, at the same time paying attention to the radio, taking into account the scenery, and considering the midterm examination I was about to take.

At that moment, I noticed that I didn't need to direct my focus to the mechanics of the task of driving anymore, or at least, not with the equal intensity of intentional concentration as before.

Driving stick had now ended up a reminiscence-handy, choreographed set of movements.

The truth is, if you drive your vehicle daily, you're enrolled in ongoing practice—exercise that enhances your talent over and over again.

There is a possibility that you might be able to pin-point a similar experience from your own reminiscences.

Try this:

Call up a memory of the first time you discovered something that required your entire focus and attention.

See the number of your senses you could combine as you recollect that experience: the way it felt, seemed, sounded, smelled, and tasted, together with the mind and emotions you experienced at the very beginning.

Until there appeared to be an opening for other inputs of awareness, how long was it before you no longer needed to pay such concentrated attention?

Mind you, if your previous memory brings you to athletic or artistic pursuits, maybe tennis, it's not unlikely that your thought maybe that you could never disengage your focus if indeed you wish to play well.

However, give yourself a simple test, see if you can create a recollection of the distinction between your first tennis lesson and everything that it encompassed, and the very first time you were able to anticipate your opponent's next move and focus on hitting the ball.

Many of us are familiar with the statement that quotes, "Practice makes perfect", which put simply means, the act of repetition transforms into perfection. Whether it's working towards being able to play the piano or, learning how to be skillful with your backhand strike, you'll find yourself in a continuous state of repetition until arriving at perfection.

**HOW MINDFULNESS HELPS YOU INTERACT WITH THE NARCISSIST**

In coping with narcissists, it's crucial to practice the art of paying attention. For instance, if you're mindfully informed of your slumped shoulders as you circulate with resignation toward another interplay with the narcissist, you're more likely to be able to engage the feasibility of positive impact.

From this standpoint of clarity, you choose to undertake a chin-up, shoulders- straight position of energy and self-belief and additionally direct your perspective in the direction of the other person's face, arms, and bodily being, reminding yourself that he's just some other member of the fascinating and imperfect human species.

With your body and thoughts nicely attuned, and with an extra practical assessment of the situation, you're unburdened of the past schemas.

Awareness fosters discovery, which in turn fosters freedom. And with that freedom comes the possibility of being accountable for how you present yourself to the world.

Instead of showing the narcissist your guilt-ridden, subjugated, or powerless, you can put forth your genuine, healthy, and grown-up self. Armed with the ownership of your present moment and connected with a sense of empathy for the narcissist's underlying disgrace and defectiveness, which he clumsily works so tough to mask, you'll have the self-belief to confront him when he crosses the line tactfully.

When it comes to schema activation or old belief systems, you will have the ability to recognise numerous important matters:

- Sudden soreness can be a signal of schema activation.
- The mind and feelings activated by way of your memories won't have anything to do with the prevailing scenario.
- You have the power of choice, once understanding that you exist in the present moment.
- You have nothing to prove and no need to hide.

As you develop a mindfully polished brain, you can stretch your thoughts, beliefs, and foresight like muscle mass honed by a commitment to a training plan or workout. And similarly, to developing muscle mass, becoming grounded inside the present moment requires ordinary exercise. With a lot to benefit from developing mindfulness, you're likely eager to get started.

The following section gives a well detailed step-by-step process for an exercise that serves in keeping your mind grounded — mindfully rooted in the present moment.

**EXERCISE: ENGAGING YOUR MINDFUL BRAIN**

As mentioned, exercise is critical to growing new abilities.

Make a commitment to carving out 5 minutes for yourself twice a day to engage with the following exercise.
Of course, adding extra time to every practice will make your experience more effective and could help to lock in your newly developed thought patterns.

You need not look out for a quiet area; you can try this exercise almost anywhere.
You can practice the exercise with your eyes open or shut. Closing your eyes allows for a deeper and more profound rendezvous with your senses; however, maintaining them open is also fine.
Read through the directions several times to get yourself up to speed with the technique. You can also make a recording of the instructions to play until your mindfulness exercise turns into second nature.

Direct your interest to your breath, and without force, simply keep the natural tempo of your breath and awareness on each of the subsequent steps:

With the primary breath, observe the rise and fall of your stomach.
With the second breath, pay attention to the expansion and contraction of your lungs.
With the third breath, sense the cool air coming through your nostrils as you breathe in, and experience the warmth of the air as you exhale.
Repeat the above method three times, noticing the upward push and fall of your abdomen, your lungs increasing and contracting, and the temperature of the air as you inhale and exhale.

If your eyes are open, visually note the space you're occupying. If they're closed, conjure up an imaginary environment.

Label what you see: the colour, length, shape, measurement, and motion of things that surround you.

Notice the sounds within your environment. Allow them to enter your auditory recognition precisely and without judgment.

Label everyone, from the roaring lyrics of the lawnmower through your window to the rambling medley of youngsters' voices. Become aware of even the most subtle of sounds: the whistle of the breath upon exhale, the quiet ticking of the clock, or the faint hum coming from your computer sitting on your desk.

Invite your nasal passages to enrol in your practice, sensing out the scents within the air.

Direct your attention towards the sensations created by things your body is in touch with. Notice your apparel against your skin, a breeze brushing your face, the texture of the floor or firmness of the cushion you're sitting on, the sensation of the floor below your feet or the sand between your toes.

Turn your attention to your inner thoughts, the arena underneath the surface of your pores and skin. If possible, engage in a few easy stretches followed by complete and full breaths. Commencing with the crown of your head, slowly scan your complete body from top to bottom, which includes your face, neck, limbs, hands, and toes.

Take notice of the sensations within your muscle groups: fatigue, tightness, tingling, pain, numbness, energy, queasiness, or weakness, for example.

Be aware of any emotional responses rising within. You may observe that your inner sensations emit a resonance of disappointment, worry, or anger. Just observe this, label it, and allow your attention to rest upon it quietly, acknowledging it without judgement.

Try to preserve a stance of openness and equanimity, which means that you ask yourself to undertake this exercise without predictions or predilections crowding your mind. Your thoughts will try and seduce you away from your practice. When that takes place, simply note them, label them, pay attention to them, and let them move on.

If thoughts like "This is foolish", "How will any of this make a difference?" flow inward, without a doubt note when you have a thought, and remember that this thought is a judgment. Allow yourself to acknowledge the thought and then let it go, bringing back your focus to your practice.

If schema thoughts invade (as an example, nothing will ever assist me in getting my needs met; I'm destined to be emotionally lonely and unfulfilled), use the technique of observing, assessing, figuring out, and differentiating already defined in the previous chapter.

Note that you're having a similar thought and examine whether or not it is related to an old thought pattern or schema. If so, discover or label it and acknowledge where the information is coming from. (For instance, Okay, I got it. I realise this is my emotional deprivation schema that reasons me to sense the pain and lonely child within me who didn't get the affection and empathy she needed.) Differentiate it by announcing. Then permit it to pass and return to your practice.

Some thoughts, particularly the ones related to schemas, can be unremitting. Your breath is your grounding force. It lightly returns you to your practice when you become swept away by the turbulence within your mind. When you discover yourself distinctly distracted, return your focus to your respiration within the manner defined at the start of the exercise, noticing the rise and fall movement of your stomach, your lungs increasing and contracting, and the temperature of the air as you inhale and exhale.

## THE REWARDS OF MINDFULNESS

Creating a practice of intentional recognition and discovery can unwrap many lovely memories. It also reveals the undesirable ones.
Remember, memories are saved within the mind, and as well as the body, and that they may be released by any of the limitless amounts of sensory stimuli.
Fortunately, as your attention becomes greatly attuned and conscious, you will be able to comfortably distinguish between reality and fiction, and among thoughts that are out-of-date and that those that are momentarily present.

In his persevering attempt to shed light and communicate the power of the brain, Dan Siegel explains that, in an attentive nation, the mind is capable of reflective cognisance, allowing you to differentiate your emotions, thoughts, and sensations, and additionally combine them in the sum of your thoughts and body. Without mindful awareness, you operate out of the default territory of automatic mental pastime. The mind is reactive, now not always receptive (Siegel 2007).

However, as noted previously, it isn't feasible to be in a state of attentive consciousness all of the time, particularly considering the busy lives we lead.
To be flawlessly conscious, all of the time would disable our vital instinctive functionality.
Paying attention is a preference and discipline. Just as listening to the circumstance of your body through conscious ingesting and exercising might also leave you with an excellent fitness, extra power, and durability, paying interest, on purpose, to your thoughts, feelings, and sensations potentially rewards you with a built-in call, alerting you to pleasant moments worth capturing—and obvious distortions really worth discarding, particularly when in reference to the narcissist in your life.

# The Four Masks of the Narcissist and How to Deal with Them

Now that you have the knowledge of narcissism, a custom profile of the narcissist in your existence, a properly-advanced inventory of your own schemas and coping styles, and greater mastery of your attentive and flexible brain, you're ready to move on to specific strategies for dealing with the 4 masks you're most likely to encounter while handling the narcissist in your existence: the show-off, the bully, the entitled one, and the addictive self-soother.

**THE SHOW-OFF**

When dealing with the show-off, understand that you're in the company of someone who hungers for the adoration and envy of others. He can be overly conceited or covertly captivating and self-effacing. He suffers from a sense of invalidity and undesirability but may not be aware of it. He has found out that if he's able to impress you, he'll be able to nourish the starvation and extinguish his disgrace quickly. He seems to have little interest in you aside from the praise and admiration you provide.

With your natural interaction with the present moment, proceed to ignore his apparent solicitations and as a substitute, provide fantastic commentaries for the easy and normal niceties of the interplay.

For instance, let's pretend that the narcissist is your friend Vanessa. Instead of saying, as you commonly would, "Oh, Vanessa, I just don't recognise how you do all of it. What a great lady you're," you can streamline your emphasis on normal matters: "Vanessa, I recognise that you made this lunch date for us. It's exceptional, and to be remembered." Focus on considerate, unadorned kindnesses rather than the excellent, and over the top actions.

Say she's simply been requested to chair the sanatorium's annual fundraising gala. It's the who's who of the community and a social extravaganza. Following her blow-through account of how they invited her to manage based totally on her upstanding popularity, poise, and exemplary public relations competencies, you could respond with "How incredible and highly demanded are you, Vanessa, to be part of something with a view to assist those who will enjoy the donations to the clinic. Good luck with it."
You candidly and thoroughly steer clear of the traps set through your schemas and don't allow yourself to be blinded by the outrageous glare of her 14-karat ego. Furthermore, by doing so, at the same time as you unwaveringly take pleasure in your own clarity, know that your frank responses would possibly even reach the part of Vanessa that actually longs to be customary without the weight of grandiloquently proving herself.

**THE BULLY**

When handling the bully, comprehend that you're within the court of a person who has an inflexible mistrust for human beings and their reasons. He's nervous that others will attempt to manipulate him, make an idiot of him, or take gain of him. He believes that nobody should simply care about him, given his history of emotional voids and his deep sense of disgrace and inadequacy. He protects himself with the aid of being important and controlling others. To obtain his craved experience of importance and authority, he must make sure that you feel susceptible, powerless, and perhaps even silly.

With your new-found governance of the present moment and newly obtained insights, you are poised with self-belief. You look him in the eye and carefully proceed to allow him to realise what his phrases and actions made you go through.

For instance, let's say that the narcissist is Brad, a colleague who's disenchanted about a painting you've just submitted. You might possibly say, "I hope you understand, Brad, that it's very troublesome and, frankly, unacceptable for you to speak to me in that tone of voice, criticising my paintings because they don't measure up to your expectations. I can recognise when you're upset or even annoyed, and I don't find it charming. Nevertheless, you don't need to be mean-spirited about it. I don't assume you want to harm me, but you now and again have a way of identifying as overly important."

Or let's say that the narcissist is Joe, who just slipped into bully mode because of a perceived lack of attention from you at an event. You may say, "Joe, I care about how you feel, and I definitely don't intend to upset you.
"I can't remember the fact that you get dissatisfied when I'm distracted, and that you'd like me to be more attentive.
It's your responsibility to tell me that, not curse at me or call me names. I don't care about you or your feelings when you do this. It isn't helpful to us, and it simply isn't acceptable to me."

In both of these scenarios, you've bypassed your former inclination just to give in, apologise, counterattack, or run away and cry. Wrapped in the comforting embrace of your sturdy inner advocate, you're clothed in courage and integrity.

**THE ENTITLED ONE**

When managing the entitled one, understand that you're dealing a person who feels that he or she will be able to make up their own set of rules and that they can have whatever they want, whenever they want it.

He behaves as if he is special and feels that he deserves to be treated in a superior way. He doesn't understand the sentiment of give-and-take.

He has trouble being on the receiving end of the word "no" and never appears to feel any regret for his frequently pushy and traumatic moves. He isn't interested in the emotions of others and doesn't feel or recognise the sentiment of empathy.

With your steady grasp of the present moment, you gently emerge from the heat rising in your face, take a breath, steady your nerves, and proceed to let the narcissist know the real deal.

For example, let's say the narcissist is your friend Leanne, who's joining you for dinner. In her usual fashion, she arrived thirty-five minutes late without calling to let you know. The restaurant has a policy that you can't be seated until the entire party has arrived, so you've been waiting at the bar, watching the tables fill. Leanne struts in with no apology and no explanation, and when she's told that it will be a while before the two of you can be seated, she angrily expresses her utter annoyance to the manager regarding this "ludicrous" policy. You're embarrassed by the loud and self-righteous scene she's making and upset by her total lack of respect for you and the value of your time.

This isn't the only time you've observed yourself wishing to be invisible while Leanne throws her predictable, entitled tirades. Your usual stance has been to stand back and smile shyly and apologetically for her rude and embarrassing behaviour.

However, this time you call her aside and say, "Leanne, that is uncomfortable and embarrassing"." It's additionally disappointing when you don't seem to have any regard at all for my feelings and act as though it's perfectly okay to do as you please, even when it has a bad impact on me. It's amazing to have that sort of savvy in certain situations. But it isn't cool to push me and my emotions aside. I realise that you'll be too disenchanted to speak about anything, this moment, and I advocate that we postpone our dinner. I'm open to speaking about this after you've had an opportunity to relax."

Bravo! No cowering, no making excuses for her, no letting her off the hook one more wasted time.

**THE ADDICTIVE SELF-SOOTHER**

When dealing with an addictive self-soother, understand that you're dealing with a person who is in a state of unknowing avoidance. The insupportable discomfort associated with his unrecognised loneliness, disgrace, and disconnection, pushes him to seek cover and hide whenever the highlight isn't casting its shimmering glow upon him. He is prone to be engrossed in workaholism, food binges, spending marathons, or voracious Internet browsing. You may go knocking. However, he will never come out of his hiding place. He can't risk being seen au natural, with all of his emotions, needs, and longings revealed.

You're expected to pander to his selective emotional abandonment and not request his presence, regardless of the emotional costs to you.

With your steady grasp of the present moment, you remind yourself that he doesn't hide behind this mask on purpose and that it isn't your fault that he's frequently detached. You act with a sense of responsibility for yourself and your role in the relationship, especially if this is a meaningful one.

For example, let's say the narcissist is your husband, Al, and he's deeply entrenched in one of his workaholic episodes. You proceed to thoughtfully confront him, saying, "I know how important your work is to you, Al, and I appreciate how your ambition and dedication have provided us with financial security and lovely opportunities. But I miss you, and I'm concerned that you might be pushing yourself harder than necessary. It's difficult for me to sit back and watch without sharing my concern and sense of loss with you. I'd like to talk about it and see if we can come up with a compromise. Please don't dismiss me or say that I just don't get it. This is truly important to me. If we can't reach an answer that satisfies both of our desires, I want to search for professional help."

No longer tossing in the towel or apologising on your intended lack of information on the subject of his career, you firmly but thoughtfully reach in to pull him from the darkness of the lonely place he inhabits.

# Exercise For Emotional Triggers

Exercise: Why the Narcissist Triggers You
See if you can find those schemas that most accurately represent the themes of your life. Keep in mind that for it to be an early maladaptive schema, it should have roots within your childhood or youth. And, even though it may lay dormant through a whole lot of your life, it's pertinent enough that you're feeling it acutely as you examine it now.
Go ahead and list your schemas on a piece of paper.

With an awareness of your schemas firmly in mind, proceed with the following exercise. Because it involves a guided visualisation, you'll need to read through it first to familiarise yourself with the steps before actually doing them.

Find a calm and relaxing place where you won't be interrupted and sit comfortably. Close your eyes for a moment. Try to recall a painful childhood memory involving one of your caregivers, a sibling, or someone from your peer group. Assign a part of you to act as a sentry— remaining keenly watchful of your feet firmly planted on the ground, safely anchored to this moment, here and now—so that you can permit yourself to gently look back and notice the thoughts, feelings, and sensations that emerge as you call up this difficult event.

What happened during this painful event?
How did you deal with it?
Can you recall what you wish had happened at that time?
What were your deepest longings?

If recalling the experience becomes difficult or painful, remind yourself that you are only remembering.

Take a gradual, deep breath after which you slowly exhale completely. Blank out the picture of that past occasion, but pounder on the thoughts, emotions, and sensations that fill your mind and body. Keep them with you, allowing your tender and gentle breath to caress any painful associations etched at the partitions of your thoughts.

Now that you've honed a recognition of troublesome thoughts, emotions, and sensations, and learnt how your breath can help ease their effect, call up a picture of the narcissist to your existence. See if you can zoom in on a tough, feeling, or stressful encounter. Make the photo as vibrant as feasibly possible in your mind. Pay attention to the thoughts, feelings, and physical responses that resonate as this charged scenario unfolds within you.

If you can manage the outcome, what you desire might show up? What are your innermost longings?

Take a couple of slow, gentle breaths, in and out, then open your eyes and give yourself a moment to become fully reengaged with your surroundings. Say thank you to the part of you that kept you safely grounded so that you could make the journey.

After you complete the practice, compare the thoughts, emotions, and physical sensations associated with the first image—your memory from childhood—with those of the second. Was there a shift, or were they consistent? The difference between your experience of the two visualisations indicates the degree to which your capacity to observe, assess, identify, and differentiate has emerged.

Turning your awareness toward the internal experience during these scenarios also allows you to measure the strength of your schemas and how entrenched old, maladaptive coping methods are when activated by current conditions.

When you compare your experience in those situations, do you see any patterns?
How have your longings gotten modified due to that childhood experience, if at all?
What do you continue to long for?
What keeps you from getting those desires met?

There are loads to recall here. You might also wish to make an effort to jot down about your thoughts and feelings to help you sort through your emotions.
Doing so can also be beneficial in the future, allowing you to gauge your progress.

In conclusion, when you make an overall observation of your schemas, you should ask yourself, Do I feel reasonably assured that I have precisely and accurately located those important life stories? —What about the ones that may be implicitly interfering with your own interpersonal skills?

If so, good for you. If not, don't worry. This is a complex task, and you may have multiple layers of history and behavioural patterns to unfold.

## Recognising Your Own Pitfalls

Now that you've sharpened your knowledge of the origins of narcissism, the ways it exhibits, and schemas associated to narcissism, let's aim the lens toward you, the person on the receiving end of the relationship. When under the narcissist's talisman, you may not be able to see what is occurring inside your psyche and body plainly. You may feel worthless and unsatisfied with your methods of dealing with this troublesome person. You're not alone in finding it challenging to communicate with a narcissist. I've encountered countless people in similar situations, regularly asking the same questions:

What's with me? Am I solely a masochist? How can I let myself to be so misled?
Why am I so attracted to these complex people? Am I being penalised?
How do these trying people perpetually find me? Do I have "mug" inscribed on my forehead? Why can't I just articulate and tell him to…

It can be challenging to evaluate toxic synergies during the initial phase of any relationship, especially if you're only in the narcissist's presence from time to time. Even when it appears clear that he is a bit disagreeable, you may have grown up with the message "Too bad; just deal with it!" embedded in your brain, particularly if the narcissist in your life happens to be an executive figure, such as a business owner, director, or educator, or even a romantic spouse. You aren't stupid, nor are you being disciplined, and you unquestionably don't have a self-defeating emblem ornamented on your forehead.

The narcissist's attraction and wit can be very hypnotising, prompting you to be magnanimous when he's out of line. You're attracted to this person because he is charming in some ways.

It can be challenging to speak up. The prices may seem too great, and if you've been part of the relationship for a while, you've been well tutored in the art of discretion—or, rather, biting your tongue.

# PART VI COMFORT ZONES: THE TRIALS OF LIVING WITH AND REMODELLING YOUR HABITS

Despite the worn-out bottoms, inadequate support, and hideous appearance of our comfy old shoes, we choose to retain them because they have come to serve us well, customised by the memory of the action of the heel, and each individual toe. We feel we can survive long walks in these shoes due to their familiar fit.

This is also the quandary with our relationships and our methods of associating with others. When confronted with a challenging circumstance, you're destined to rely on what you recognise—the unconscious patterns programmed into your brain's reply system.

It's only when the "sole comes undone" in a relationship, or the sadness becomes too great, that we begin to encounter grief, stress, and fear.

Once things become this uncomfortable, you may be amenable to break out of your comfort zone and fix those old shoes, or perhaps throw them out and try something different, even if it's awkward at first.

Your early encounters of the world—from operating the landmass of your cradle with guests' faces hovering above you, to scaling the incline of your mother's lap on a quest of comfort, to bartering the playground in search of acceptance and inclusion—contributed many thoughts and sensations that you have gathered and deposited in your memory archives for future reference.

Retrieval of these mementoes, such as what might occur when you cry, smile, or show anxiety or agitation, and what to do about it, wants little effort given the repetitious nature of so much of our existence and how foreseen the results often are.

From our early years as feeble little people, we are informed by the anxiety of travels filled with innumerable letdowns and emotional bargainings, but in the process, we become adorned with a compass for survival.

We learn swiftly what we can anticipate from the world, from the people in it, and from ourselves. The well-designed structural landscape of the brain is widespread, accommodating space for beliefs, opinions, behaviours, and physical sensations. It contains countless rooms for our inhabitance. Experience is the concierge of the mind, discreetly leading us from room to room.

## Reasons the Narcissist Triggers You

Take a few minutes to think back at the schemas defined in the previous chapters, and once again recognise your schemas. If you're like most people, you'll find that numerous of the schemas seem to fit. It's very popular for schemas to transpire in groups.

Some of the groupings most frequent among people in relationships with narcissists are defectiveness and ruthless standards; distrust and subjugation; and abandonment, emotional withholding, and self-sacrifice.

Let's take a closer look at those clusters.

**DISTRUST AND SUBJUGATION**

You might find yourself identifying with the distrust and subjugation schemas if your inner autobiography recounts the story of a child who got taken advantage of or harmed. As such, your response to manipulative or cruel people is to subjugate yourself by tucking in your emotions and doing what you're advised to do.

If you had no one to guard you when you were a child, this might have been the only sensible route to survive. Now that you're an adult, when the narcissist in your life becomes dominating or difficult or puts you down with judgment and culpability, your old memories are ignited, along with customary responses.

Your shielding mechanisms cause you to react to the power and abuse by closing down and doing what you're instructed to do. Nevertheless, there's a predicament with your inner guard system: the long-choreographed actions are in urgent need of a tune-up or overhaul.

Rooted in the past, your customary beliefs and responses are antiquated, yet they apprehend you and keep you hostage. As a result, you lose your speech and relinquish your rights.

**DEFECTIVENESS AND UNRELENTING STANDARDS**

If you have a mixture of the defectiveness and ruthless standards schemas, this might be because you were made to feel unlovable, incomplete, or defective as a child. In acknowledgement, you may have made your best endeavour to be reliable and adequate and to get it right in order to circumvent critique, achieve recognition, and enjoy loving care. In the present moment, when the narcissist in your life is critical or restricting, you work as arduously as you can to be the ideal friend, spouse, co-worker, or family member. Regrettably, you're dancing to a faraway drummer within an orchestra of recollections playing antiquated tunes.

**ABANDONMENT, EMOTIONAL NEGLECT, AND SELF-SACRIFICE**

You might have a mixture of abandonment, emotional withholding, and self-sacrifice schemas if you grew up sensing that there was no one you could honestly count on, that the people you loved could leave you, or that they would never truly appreciate you or give you the love, kindness, and comfort you required. You may have reached these beliefs due to the volatility of an alcoholic parent, the death of a caregiver, a breakup, or possibly a parent who was too pessimistic about nourishing you appropriately.

Through the unification of personality and occurrence, you may have put your requirements aside to focus on taking custody of others. If you seemed like a burden to your parents and were sympathetic to their upsets and expectations, you probably strived hard to please them, demanding for little in replacement and appreciating whatever scraps came your way.
An ever-presiding feeling of blame eclipsed any bitterness about being bereaved or rejected.

As a consequence, when dealing with the narcissist in your life you delicately walk the tight, narrow path, retaining your own necessities hidden away. Nervous of losing him or lighting his short fuse, you give in, allowing him and surrendering your personal needs. That is, until your knowledgeable and desirous mind tunes in, charging you with bitterness and propelling you into your own "what about me" diatribe.
Regrettably, this sets you up for his spirited response to the pains and yearnings you attempted to voice, and—you retreat to your familiar post of the guilt-ridden supplier.

## Cultivating an Authentic Voice

Of course, it may be that when you find yourself provoked or triggered by difficult intercommunications with you know who, you fight back by bullying, commanding, or intimidating. And while you seem to own an intimidating voice, the primary adversary in your battle is only an illusion: the enemy arising from your memory's archives. You feel your buttons being pushed, and you counter-attack or get protective. Nevertheless, there is a distinction among taking a stand for yourself—using an authoritative and authentic voice against abuse, manipulation, and coercion—and protecting yourself with hatred, contempt, and self- righteousness.

**EXERCISE: THE BLAME**

Are you eager to take on the responsibility of change without the culpability—to admit that even if your schemas aren't your mistake, you are accountable for your behaviour now, as a grown-up? Though it may seem a bit scary or overpowering, this also unlocks the door to the potential for transmutation. This activity will help you explore your own schemas and coping methods and identify healthy and positive ways of reacting to substitute old models of behaviour. This will be innately good for you, and there's a good possibility that your open communication will help enhance your relationship with the narcissist. In this activity, you'll also analyse any leverage you might have for capturing the awareness of the narcissist in your life and positioning that person for reform. Here's an illustration:

Your schemas: Abandonment, defectiveness, altruism, and subjugation.
Consequences of your schemas: I take the culpability, feel weak, and think that it's better to put my needs to one side and be quiet than to speak up, get it wrong, and perhaps end up alone.
Your coping methods: Giving in and bypassing.
The accuracy: It isn't my responsibility. We both play a part in the dispute. I am competent of being responsible, and secondly, I'm already so lonely because I don't have knowledge of self, an opinion, or a quintessential connection with my partner.

Wholesome assertive message: I won't be treated in this way. It's unacceptable, even if it isn't your aim to harm me.

Leverage: I recognise that my partner doesn't want to lose me. I'm prepared to start conversing about the possibility of leaving—not as intimidation, but as a vital choice if things don't shift between us.

Using the arrangement set forth in that example, take a new piece of paper and write about your personal schemas and coping methods, then examine the truth of the situation. Take some time to produce a healthy positive message—one that neither quails before the narcissist in your life nor strikes that person spitefully. Lastly, take some time to reflect what advantage you might use to secure the narcissist in making modifications to enhance your relationship.

## The Ability to Discover and Transform

Without the unlikely interference of magic, the options for fixing conflicts in relationships are limited: finishing the relationship, adhering with the status quo, embracing new dysfunctional exemplars, or talking it out in a salubrious way. The latter of these is unmistakably best if you wish to remain in the relationship, but it demands an exhausting dedication, even when both individuals are fully engaged in the process of transformation. But rest ensured: While the trial may seem daunting, the opportunities for restoration are true.

The brain is able to change, and consequently, our personalities are malleable and open to evolving as well. Specialists in mental health, along with those who investigate the brain, recommend that one pathway to reform may come from attuned listening and authentic self-expression in the context of a conscious, and present state of mind. Dan Siegel utilises the term "contingent communication" to illustrate this method: "In contingent communication, the recipient of the information listens with an open mind and with all his or her senses. Her response is reliant on what was truly communicated, not on a predetermined and resolute mental model of what was expected".

Siegel goes on to explain the nature of "feeling sensed" in reference to the parent-child connection: "When we send out a signal, our brains are perceptive to the replies of others to that signal. The replies we receive become rooted in the neural maps of our core sense of self. The replies of others are not simply mirrors of our own signals but combine the essence of the other person's viewpoint, which makes sense of our communication. In this manner, children come to feel felt: they come to feel as if their mind subsists in the mind of their parent".

What a soothing connection—to feel truly "understood," to sense that you are held correctly and securely in the mind of another.

Think about it, who truly gets you?

## CONCLUSION

Within the setting of "felt" attachments, we are provided with the opportunity to achieve mental and emotional transformations that span to new understandings and behaviours concerning self-worth and our relationships with others. These connections offer us the opportunity of developing new habits and liberating ourselves from unconscious reflexes associated with the past. So, the task is to build this sort of reciprocity with the narcissist in your life, whether that somebody is a supervisor, coworker, family member, acquaintance, companion, husband, or partner.

Regrettably, these last two are normally the most opposing to change, given the immensity of the significance of the relationship and how heartily entrenched your schemas maybe for two of you. But by ascertaining a more "felt" attachment, you unlock the door to restoring your sense of self, and to the opportunity of using your collection of skills to enhance and change your relationship with the narcissist or, if that isn't viable, defining the relationship or even finishing it.

To this end, the subsequent chapters will help you intensify your awareness, secure your courage, and support your energy while developing the abilities you need for producing productive results when dealing with the narcissist in your life.

# PART VII EMPATHY

Even if you've concluded that your narcissist doesn't fall into the dangerous class, being in his company when he's in his less-than-charming, Mr Hyde form can feel like being with an adversary.

Schemas get triggered, leaving you sensing woozy, inarticulate, or at the end of your tether. These personalities seem to be capable of sucking the energy directly out of the room.

Being mad and fed up momentarily thickens your skin to the narcissist's demeaning behaviour, or so it appears. But bearing anger can become tiresome after a while.

Before you know it, the exhaustion can bring you right back to feeling unprepared and impotent. So, you abdicate to the narcissist's aggressive manoeuvres and wait for him to ultimately, return to his delightfully sweet and hospitable mode.

Nevertheless, with your new mindfulness and conversational skills, this needn't be dynamic. You can persist more unyielding and steadfast in the centre of the commotion. You need not jeopardise your values or honour in the face of the narcissist's commands. The bottom line is that you have rights, strong needs and wants, and intrinsic value.

But to advance your interpersonal effectiveness and accomplish more fulfilling outcomes, you'll need more than a sound mind and attuned intuitive balance; you need to understand who the narcissist is genuinely. You require more than a mental literacy in his problems and life narrative; you also need emotional knowledgeability in his internal world. In other terms, you need to feel what his sense of reality is like. It's similar to sensing his mind inside of yours. This isn't mind reading; this is what is more commonly referred to as empathy.

Before you continue, one serious note: This approach is inadvisable with anyone who makes you feel insecure or hurt. That calls for a totally
separate methodology, often demanding exit tactics and protection plans. If the narcissist in your life is destructive, cruel, or endangers your security in any way, please seek support instantly.

## The difference between Empathy and Sympathy

There seems to be an abundant amount of confusion when it comes to the word "empathy." Countless people use it reciprocally with "sympathy." And while both may transpire in the circumstances of witnessing another person's distress or pleasure, the two are considerably distinct from one another, and in ways that are extremely relevant in any conversation of narcissism.
So, let's take a second to distinguish empathy from sympathy.

Empathy is a capability to comprehend the experience of another, emotionally, psychologically truly, and seldom even physically. It doesn't signify that you undoubtedly agree with, approve, or encourage the other person's emotions and behaviour, solely that you understand it in a "sensed" way.
In an empathic disposition, you endure the thoughts, emotions, and sentiments of another within your own consciousness and body. It's as if you can feel the person's occurrence resonating inside yourself. You are wholly harmonised.

Here's an example:
Let's say a friend and co-worker appears at work visibly shaking and unsettled. She progresses to report a car accident she nearly had while making her way to work. She can still

envision the truck rolling toward her and the second in which she directed her vehicle toward the hard-shoulder to evade being struck. She then recounts how she ceased to offer relief to another driver who wasn't as fortunate and was hit badly. She becomes teary as she addresses the what-ifs of the circumstance and how fortunate she feels to be alive and unharmed. Apprehensively laughing, she says, "Picture, being so content to be here at work on a Monday morning." You tell her how pleased you are, too, that she's safe. You state that you can only presume how petrifying it must have been.

You envision the event as she expresses it. You entertain the outline in your mind, simultaneously with all of the what-ifs. You sense your own body tensing-up as she explains the noise of horns blasting and the force of the truck smashing into the other vehicle just a couple of feet from where she had halted. You sense your heart rate raising at the notion of a phone call stating that your friend had been seriously injured or killed. You might even recollect the experience of a comparable situation in your personal life. When she declares that she'll be alright and just requires a few minutes to catch her breath and drink some water, you can fully feel her urge to attempt a sense of peacefulness and relaxation; it emanates within you too. This is what is known as empathy.

While sympathy demands this sort of empathic consciousness or perception, it goes farther. Sympathy is a radiating urge to comfort, aid, and mitigate the discomfort and distress of another. It's rooted in a profound sense of empathic feeling where you have seized a precise sense of the other person's occurrence, accompanied by sympathy for the other person's trouble. Compassion is the inclination to move further beyond empathy for another person's pains; it means feeling forced to extend courtesy, to do something about the person's endeavour, to bring comfort or healing.

Travelling back to the earlier example, with compassion you would hold your friend to reassure her and say something similar to "Please, let me fetch the water for you. Why don't you just clean up and then sit and take a few calm minutes for yourself? And please let me know if there's anything more I can do, even if you simply want to talk."
With compassion, it's complicated to walk away without wanting, assuming, or doing some sort of plan or move for relief.

When it comes to appropriating empathy and compassion in your involvement with a narcissist, the difficulty can be daunting, given how infrequently narcissists exhibit their vulnerability. Yet the capacity to endure empathy and even maybe compassion for this troubling and confused person is just the talent you need for obtaining more satisfying results in interactions—and probably a more gratifying relationship.

## Feeling "Sensed"

Salubrious development of the child into an adult is dependent upon a parent or caregiver presenting attuned emotional reciprocity—in other terms, empathy. As a child gazes up into her parent's eyes for support or validation, the parent consciously echoes back a comprehension of her occurrence, whether happiness, despair, uncertainty, or anguish. The parent receives and verifies the child's emotions or requirements and helps her make sense of what's occurring within her: "Of course, I know it's very scary to see beasts on your bedroom door, and you don't want to be there alone with them. Let's go and see if maybe it's just those stupid shadows, playing in the luminescence, that crept in anew."
When this necessity for attuned reciprocity isn't satisfactorily met, the child's experience of feeling misinterpreted, inconspicuous, insignificant, unwanted, or even embarrassed of

unmet yearning for connection can lead to unpleasant self-labels, such as "vulnerable," "stupid," or "unlovable," and self-defeating behaviour patterns, such as aloofness, avoidance, or aggressiveness.

Sensing that others understand you are a profoundly underestimated human need, and it's imperative for the advancement of empathic consciousness, which is vital for wholesome emotional and interpersonal growth.

A key feature of narcissism is endeavouring to feel visible but in a maladaptive fashion. In the deficiency of feeling "gotten," narcissists search for validation, primarily in respect to their achievement. They fight to receive exclusive entitlements as evidence of their victory and extraordinariness.

They also strive to secure absolute authority and necessitate emotional sovereignty of themselves, procuring a sense of control from not necessitating anyone.

There is a deep pit of guilt connected to their quashed but very human desire to be recognised, noticeable, loved and trusted. Their unmet need for attuned soulful connection and their incipient knowledge of their own rhetoric leaves them without passage to actions of empathy with others.

Rather than attuning to others, the narcissist remains hooked up in the distracting pursuance of approval: How am I looking? She genuinely likes me. I think I hammered it. I think I awed him. I wonder if they love what I just said. This selfish "all about me" focus limits the narcissist from truly engaging in synergies, much less encountering or communicating empathy. As a consequence, those he associates with are left feeling meaningless, hollow, and frustrated.

Nevertheless, with the exclusion of people suffering from specific forms of head injury, almost all humans hold the capability for empathy. Cultivating empathy in a narcissist isn't an unattainable mission—but it is complex.

It demands dependable professional help from a specialist who understands narcissism and is qualified in working with this group.

Regrettably, getting narcissists to consent to go to therapy is customarily difficult. It takes leverage—building significant consequences, such as losing someone or something meaningful, and implementing those consequences if they don't get an assistant.

As mentioned earlier, empathy doesn't fundamentally mean agreeing with others or excusing their actions; it simply needs understanding. To this end, we psychologically and emotionally conjure up an internal vision, account, or physical sensation that allows us to visualise or sense the experiences or purposes of others. We become emotionally, intellectually, and corporally engaged in composing sense out of what we perceive and apprehend, whether it's a personality in a movie, a treasured one standing before us, or possibly even the form in the mirror.

This illuminates a path to purpose and relieves us of misappropriated duty, blame, noxious anger, guilt, failure, and weakness. We must have passage to our vulnerable side in order to take in the grief or happiness of another. This is frequently an obstacle for the narcissist.

Empathy also generates clarity and higher consciousness of what is real, releasing us from the distorted viewpoints commanded by the filters of our schemas. This opens the gateway to emotional release from biased views and useless self- defensiveness and unblocks the path toward personal transmutation.

This state of "comprehending," of emotional and mental awareness, provides much- needed insight when dealing with a narcissist. His ways of acting and relating have so much power to trigger old, schema-driven opinions and outlooks that can make you doubt the authenticity about who you are, your worth, and possibly even your capability to be in a relationship. You may lose your strength to state your opinions or feel self-conscious or less-than if your thoughts aren't as "audacious" or "skilful" as his.

Because empathy allows you to genuinely appreciate who the narcissist is and why he is that way, it's the ideal remedy, strengthening you to stand strong, hold him answerable, and not take the blame for his issues.

Best of all, you can show up in communications with him without the weight of exhausting resentment, defensiveness, or submissiveness. You perceive him. You may even feel sorry for him and might even tell him that, but you can do so without falling in and without yielding up your rights.

With experience, your empathy—your felt discernment of the narcissist's suffering—may even develop into compassion. This doesn't always occur, and of course, it depends upon how broken your heart has become, enduring the harsh and severe disturbances of narcissism.

If the wound isn't too great, you may find yourself desiring to help, support, trust, or even acquit. Sometimes this is absolutely fitting; it might even be what's needed—as long as it doesn't disrupt your primary and non-negotiable rights and needs.

## A Brief Glimpse at the Science of Empathy

In the 1980s and 1990s, neuroscientists identified an interesting type of neurons that are stimulated both when we perform a specific activity, such as gripping a bowl or a knife or even grinning or scowling, and when we observe someone else operating the same action.

It's practically like the brain is reacting as if we are observing our own appearance in a mirror. Hence, these brain cells are termed mirror neurons.

Recent neuroscience studies into empathy using patterns perceived in functional magnetic resonance imaging scans propose that meaning and individual design, including biology, character traits, and emotional elements, play a part in recognising the extent to which a person can obtain empathic awareness.

Evidently, connecting and attuned replies are seldom dominated by the impulse to seek vengeance or correct, particularly when perceptions of unfairness or deliberate abuse are present.

What does this report to us about the narcissist?

Perhaps his need to guard himself is holding him back from painstakingly unpleasant emotions, particularly those that make him feel as though he doesn't satisfy your wants.

When you tearfully reveal your discomfort and solitude, his displeasure, schemas, and bolted emotional status keep him practically blindfolded. Incapable of seeing and sensing your emotions, he is saved from feeling his own vulnerability. Instead, he promptly flips into a holier-than-thou mode of exasperated sighs and dismissive comebacks.

You may even discover yourself on the receiving end of a reciprocating acknowledgement that stems from his sense that you're deliberately attempting to make him feel unsatisfactory about himself.

**MIRRORING THE OTHER**

Shared human encounters are possibilities for a new enlightenment, and wisdom presents a gateway to liberation from false ideas, disturbances, and self-defeating practices.

Once our subjective vision is clear, we can see and sense the forces and fights others experience. When this clarity and attendant empathy appear in a relationship, people transform into mirrors for one another.

We all flourish on seeing an authentic portrayal of ourselves displayed and contained in mind and heart of a notable other, even when we don't yield the same point of view.

We all want to feel appreciated—not judged, neglected, or depreciated—for who we are and how we encounter and react to the world, even if it may appear ridiculous sometimes. This is what creates a foundation that's sturdy enough to resist the weighty and uncomfortable triggers that we eternally face in our most meaningful relationships.

# Deep Within

Brace yourself! Here comes the real test.

Many people who are dealing with a narcissist have heard someone say, "You must illuminate the torch and pave the way in order for transformation to transpire," suggesting they must extend empathy in order to obtain it.

However, I also assert that they shouldn't have to bear that torch endlessly; the narcissist must reciprocate and become perceptive.

Throughout, you must thoroughly measure and judge progress and decide when enough is enough. You continually have the liberty to alter your mind and make an alternative choice.

Think about it though: If the narcissist is someone who plays a vital role in your life, it may be beneficial to attempt to make it work or to assure yourself that you've done all you could before quitting. And now that you've decided to skim the autobiography aisle of your emotional archives, rather than the schema-triggered fantasy aisle, you can better appreciate the makeup of both the narcissist and yourself and remain judiciously rooted in authenticity.

Placing yourself in the narcissist's position means attempting to sense and genuinely feel his internal world. Particular methods can help you do this. For instance, when the narcissist starts to address you piercingly, you could superimpose the face of a desolate and unloved little boy over that of the developed man before you. As you imagine the face of that child, try to visualise his background: his uncomfortable feelings, his sense of defectiveness and humiliation, his isolation and emotional void, the improbable but inescapable circumstances he had to face to gain recognition, love, or validation—maybe sometimes confusingly intertwined with the message that he was the greatest, most glorious, and most ideal boy in the world.

You muster up your empathy and embrace the boy that the man in front of you cannot stand to feel conscious.

When reparenting the narcissist, importance is put upon nurturing the isolated and deprived child buried within, doing so with both caring and direction. Confined reparenting involves empathy and placing limits, occurrences the narcissist didn't have as a child, forming ways he can nurture and care for this piece of himself. This fixes damaging schemas and restructures the way the child is cradled in remembrance.

You'll find that conjuring up empathy and perhaps even compassion for the child within the narcissist is a remarkably valuable mechanism for sustaining an even keel. Try to apprehend and firmly secure a snapshot of the defenceless child within your soul while the adult in front of you is once again nonchalantly stuttering about one subject or another.

This will fuel you with the understanding that what typically motivates his drama is a need to circumvent the feelings of the little child behind the uproars—the vulnerability he sees as pitiful and pathetic.

You can look upon and sense that child as clearly frightened, depressed, and bereaved, even if he was seldom spoiled too.

Without an intelligent awareness, the adult narcissist is getting his signals from the child within—the child with the vast assortment of unpleasant early encounters that plague his interpersonal relationships in the present moment.

Here's a practical tip: Try to get a photograph of the narcissist as a kid. This can be very serviceable in producing empathy or compassion. It's also an excellent idea to have a photo of yourself as a child to remind you that the helpless part within you also requires your compassion and thoughtfulness.

# Retaining the Narcissist on the Hook

Loading your emotional reserve with empathy and compassion doesn't mean letting the narcissist off when he's acting negligently. While it is essential to harness your comprehension and emotional altruism, it's evenly necessary to hold the narcissist responsible when he acts egotistic, self-centred, commanding, or utterly nasty.

- Distinguishing between guilt and accountability
- Setting boundaries.
- Ascertaining the rules of mutuality.
- Encouraging optimal awareness by contributing confident feedback.

**TIME OUTS**

To secure leverage with the narcissist, you need to be listened to. If you're in a heightened position of displeasure and at the origin of a noxious verbal outflow or retreat, you may need time to sit with your feelings and deconstruct the precipitating circumstances that pushed your buttons.
Self-help books for couples and on temper management are full of recommendations to take a time-out when inundated with powerful feelings or intensification of anger. This is good information.
Time-outs can be very effective for de-escalation and reflection, and also enable the physiological consequences of the fight.

John Gottman, a globally known authority in relationships and how to prognosticate divorce, addresses the difficulties and importance of calming down before engaging in healing conversation after a rupturing experience. He states that while many adjusted and reportedly happy couples can argue without disastrous results to their relationship, couples who have a delicate association to one another fight in damaging forms and often need time to steady their fierce emotional and physiological states before subscribing to the reconstruction.

The time-out is often described as each person trying out some fleeting distance from the other, maybe by going to a separate room or taking a walk for a certain amount of time. The idea is to have a cooling-off interval before revisiting the argued issue or even just being nearby one another.

In schema therapy, we also advise that when you're triggered, and your body and mind become inundated with overwhelming or hostile feelings, it's best to seek out a makeshift refuge to catch your breath and recover your emotional durability.

But what can you do throughout this phase to help you to get comfy in your own skin again?

## BREATHE

Those soft, calming inhalations you use in your mindfulness practice can be healthful. During a time-out, settle in and devote a few minutes to feeling the ascent and descent of your abdomen, your lungs inflating and closing, the air you inhale, and the warmness of your expiration. With each breath, immerse your mind and body in pacifying tranquillity and vigorous clarity.

## FLASHCARD

Retain a flashcard or two that can serve as a prompt for classifying the schema you've fallen victim to and awakening you to the present moment. The flashcard can serve as a guide in guiding you toward more salutary responses.

One the flashcard, utilise the four steps you learned in the previous chapter (observe, assess, identify, and differentiate) and add a concluding step of scanning for fresh ways to calm yourself:

Find a Distraction.
Wholesome distractions can also help sustain your mood and calm your emotions while in the time-out phase.
Here are useful suggestions:

- Read or write poetry.
- Listen to classical music.
- Do a crossword.
- Organize.
- Make a to-do list.
- Dance or sing.
- Exercise.
- Meditate.
- Take a bath.
- Get a massage.

## The Role of Empathy in the Therapeutic Relationship

The therapist shouldn't solely be a good listener who reflectively endorses the narcissist's grievances and unyielding avoidance. The therapist must also be sturdy and able to confront the narcissist's anger or critique. If the therapist is too submissive, the narcissist will presumably dissipate a lot of time showing off, accusing, seeking validation, and possibly ridiculing the therapist. If the therapist is frightened, the narcissist will sense it, attempt to dominate the therapist, and commandeer therapy or put an end to it. And while the therapist must be aware of narcissism, she must be more than a specialist in theory; she must be trustworthy. If the therapist is too mental, there's a risk that this will augment the narcissist's contentious and disjoined coping methods.

The therapist must also have genuine regard and utilise empathy, understanding and being able to emotional reverberation with these demanding clients. This means composing an effort to undergo the internal world of the client, though not fundamentally agreeing with the client or extending empathy or sympathy. Indeed, an empathic dispute is one of the essential skills in handling these clients.

"Yes, I get that your dad sold you the advice that you were authorised to exclusive privileges. But the world doesn't operate that way, and he didn't equip you to live in this world, particularly when it comes to taking accountability for the influence of your reactions on others and enabling yourself to be absolutely loved. And I have to inform you that the way you're speaking to me now is very off-putting and disruptive. I assume it must be troublesome for people to listen to you when they're distracted by this aggressive tone."

In therapy, empathic awareness is the launching block for placing limits and holding clients answerable for unkind actions and lack of regret. Sometimes it unlocks the door to more profound investigations. Persistently pushing upon the narcissist's rebellious avoidance and emotional aloofness can help modify self-defeating patterns and unbearable emotions that have held him hostage.

Finally, the therapist must be authentic, be honest, and mindful, operating in and considering moment-to-moment experiences in the therapy contact. Narcissists have a lot of scepticism, particularly of people who care about them. Elucidating the truth through a method of discovery produces a bond that enables safety and support in the therapeutic relationship. Ultimately, the therapist must be able, to tell the truth to a narcissistic patient and placing boundaries without depreciating the client. In this way, the therapist helps reparent the client, intensifying his salubrious adult self by meeting the essential needs of the helpless part concealed within.

**CONCLUSION**

Change can be a laborious and exasperating endeavour. Not everyone is ready or prepared to change or even engaged in doing so. Fear can be a primary impediment, including anxiety of reviving the terrible feelings rooted in schemas, even if the intention is to surfeit those feelings. But given all that you've uncovered about the brain, you know that transformation is possible.

In this chapter, you've had an opportunity to see that likelihood in action. You've examined some of the most crucial implements for encouraging change: empathic confrontation, sympathy, self-advocacy, setting boundaries, and sustaining leverage.

In the final chapter of the book, I'll proceed to guide you through approaches that will further accessorise your brand-new linguistic ensemble.

# PART VIII NEW FORMS OF COMMUNICATION WITH A NARCISSIST

Every one of us has an individual way of speaking that issues from a combination of temperament and skills that are adopted and practised, funnelled through spoken and composed words, gestures, facial expressions, attitudes, and body language as a means of connecting with others.

The communication gifts mentioned in this chapter are nothing like the "gift of the gab," referring to the capacity to continue forever and on about anything. Instead, they are the advantages from genuine interaction, suitable to the context and conducted with integrity, that you can reap, both personally and interpersonally.
They are also the gifts that you give to others when you interact carefully and thoughtfully, focusing not exclusively on what you state, however, more so to how you say it. Similarly, as the expression "gift" has many different meanings, there are also gifts of communication with a narcissist on various different levels.

A gift can either be something provided to another willingly or via the act of giving. "Gift" can likewise refer to natural qualities or abilities and usually includes innate talents when used in this form. This would suggest in terms of communication that an individual has an inherent forte to touch other people's hearts and souls.

However, through training and perseverance, talent can also be created. I see talented communicators as individuals who have actively cultivated a facility to listen to their internal wisdom and make sense out of their life, just as you have been doing throughout this book. Gifted communicators understand the importance of observing, listening and examining the world beyond their own skin. With elegance, grace, and thoughtfulness, they express themselves and participate in the dialogue. The astonishing news is that this ability can all be learned.

At this point, you've learned a lot about yourself, particularly about your association with the narcissist in your life. You have obtained a fresh degree of internal wisdom. Learned and honed abilities to embrace the present moment and distinguish between fiction and reality.
You have a fresh consciousness and perhaps a heart and mind that are more empathically attuned, allowing you to peel back the narcissist's layers to discover the fragile, lonely soul at his core.

Without being defensive, you can stand up for yourself because you feel no need to defend. Without resorting to counterattack, you can create a thoughtful request. You can anticipate the probability of imperfect and even unsettling moments and acknowledge this possibility with less anxiety as you have a new set of skills to repair and mend these interactions.
The newfound realisation that none of us has the power or even the potential to change someone else makes you unburdened. However, you have established newfound self-expression techniques and attuned listening capabilities that serve to develop a beneficial impact, opening up a new space where change can take place. With your own personally crafted art of communication, you have the ability to package and share your gifts.

## Harnessing the Force

Maybe you're familiarised with the Star Wars phrase "May the Force be with you." The Jedi knights' philosophy shows that a sensitive, interplanetary energy lives within all of us, binding us together and offering us the strength to withstand opposition and create light in dark times.

I would like to propose a comparable strategy, captured by the acronym FORCE, which stands for flexibility, openness, receptivity, skill, and enlightenment.

When your mind is actively involved in this FORCE state, your interactions will be more genuine and rewarding, and you will be able to share your knowledge in a manner that sheds bright and brilliant light on darker times. Use your heightened empathy and sharp focus to manifest all of the FORCE components when interacting with hard individuals:

Flexibility: adjust your statements, concerns, and answers to satisfy the scenario. Oppose and discard inflexible and unbendable inclinations and thoughts.

Openness: Listen without judgment or preconceived desires. You enable discovery to take place by not jumping to conclusions.

Receptivity: Utilise eye contact, facial expression, and body language in combination with your words and speech tone to indicate you are willing to connect to others and invite their thoughts and emotions without coercion, disruption, or censorship.

Competence: Be a reliable and empathic listener and show clarity and sensibility with passionate and attuned listening when communicating. Be an authenticity role model and don't be inspired by obtaining recognition.

Enlightenment: Be curious. Encourage and show interest in the exchange of ideas. Create an atmosphere of mutual awareness and understanding through spoken and unspoken language, shine the light of wisdom on the darkness of ignorance, and invite others to do the same for you.

Being self-possessed allows you to take advantage of your own FORCE. But here's the irony; the art of efficient communication, which contains all of the FORCE's elements, cannot be effective if it's forced. It must develop as naturally and graciously as leaves unfold in spring.

Although it may seem hard to reach your inner resources, they do lie within. It is essential to understand that becoming self-possessed does not imply becoming selfish if you have undergone the slings and arrows of a self-sacrifice or subjugation scheme. It merely implies equalising the percentage of providing and receiving or getting off the tiresome one-way road that leads eventually to the narcissist — being self-possessed means being informed by enlightened awareness and steady trust. It implies becoming personally defined. Everything you've learned from this book, and everything you've studied from other sources of knowledge and help, will guide the way.

If your new abilities allow you to develop a satisfying and reciprocal relationship with the narcissist, you will certainly feel that a huge burden has been lifted.

One of the most significant gifts life has to offer is undoubtedly a satisfying relationship.

Furthermore, your mastery of efficient communication with the narcissist can generalise other complicated relationships into effective communication. After all, if you can adequately manage one of the planet's biggest button pushers, you can handle nearly anyone.

## Presenting Your Offerings

Throughout this book, you have gathered many tools to survive and thrive in a relationship with a narcissist. It's not going to be a simple trip, but in time, you'll learn to use these tools more appropriately and in harmony.

Your tools of detecting strategies, anticipating challenging encounters, being mindful, participating in self-reflection, directing a focus on the breath, using empathic confrontation, expanding empathy, and all the others, are built to integrate with each other to ignite your internal FORCE, strengthen your voice, and reinforce your attitude as you enter into challenging interpersonal encounters.

It's comparable to what's involved in playing tennis: you need to anticipate the actions of the other person, move to be able to react, keep your eye on the ball, modify your reaction as required, create a powerful and coherent ball contact, and follow-through, and then be prepared to do it all over again.

I have concentrated on communication abilities that are specific to the difficulties of dealing with a narcissist up to this stage. Here are a few more general communication abilities that you can use to help increase the efficiency of the skills that you have been working on:

Matching impact with purpose:
Craft what you say and how you say it so that the listener will receive it as you intended. Please remember what you wish to convey and choose words and ways to express yourself that will guarantee the message you want to deliver is received by the other person.

For instance, if you are conscious that you are very upset but would mainly like to communicate that you feel lonely, you will need to express yourself deliberately in a manner that communicates loneliness rather than anger.

Modelling:
Give an example of what you expect in return to the other person.
For instance, if you talk politely and respectfully, you're going to have a better opportunity of receiving the same appropriate response.

Having reasonable expectations:
Know your audience and what he is capable of and understand yourself and what you feel capable of in that time. Some days are better than others for engaging in the challenge of communicating on complicated issues. Know your mind and body and choose your battles thoughtfully.

Besides all the abilities and ideas, you have gathered to survive and thrive in your relationship with a narcissist, the seven communication gifts below complement your abilities and enrich all your relationships. Not only the hard ones!

Also, remember that in order to be efficient in this artful use of communication, you must come prepared with constant eye contact; a smooth, confident and clear voice; a patient ear; and, of course, the FORCE, a flexible, open, receptive, skilful and enlightened mindset.

## The Seven Artful Forms Of Communication

You give precious gifts to those you communicate with by interacting with honesty and self-disclosure. Sharing yourself and your internal strength and knowledge in this manner will also help you to strengthen your self-worth and guide the narcissist in your life to do the same, healing the insecure and broken child inside.

This further opens the door to the opportunity that your relationship will change positively.//
A particular type of artful communication is associated with each gift.//
As you model these seven arts, the narcissist can possibly become a more efficient communicator, close the circle and enable you to become the beneficiary of these same offerings.//
There are, of course, various arts of interaction, each with a supplement of gifts contained in it, but the following seven are the most important for our purposes:

1. An expression of the offering of generosity is the art of mutual respect.
2. Self-disclosure art is an expression of the offering of courage.
3. An expression of the offering of truth is the art of discernment.
4. Collaboration art is an expression of the offering of shared effort.
5. An expression of the offering of foresight is the art of anticipating clashes.
6. An expression of the offering of responsibility is the art of apology.
7. Reflective listening art is an expression of the offering of balance.

**THE ART OF MUTUAL RESPECT**

Mutual respect involves recognising differences among yourself as well as other people without negative labelling. This is the gift of generosity.//
You acknowledge the different opinion or preference of the narcissist without becoming critical, defending your stance or rejecting your own opinions.

You realise that, while there is hardly a challenge when the two of you see things eye to eye, differences can set the stage for a long, drawn-out drama.

You know that understanding something does not necessarily imply agreeing with it.

You are dedicated to understanding, compromising, and respecting the ideas, views, and wishes of each other.

In exchange, you expect the same.

## THE ART OF SELF-DISCLOSURE

Self-disclosure enables you to unburden yourself of retention reality. That's the gift of courage. Safely linked to your internal strength, you discard your usual murmur and disclose your fuller, dynamic experience to the narcissist without the use of gratuitous insult.

Although exposing your vulnerability to him often seems counterintuitive, like seeking to hug a growling dog, you've learned that his bark is a protective tool; maybe he's more like a sheep in the clothing of a wolf.

You don't divulge yourself so as to make him feel like he's an awful person, but rather to assist him in understanding the effect of his actions on you. If you are no longer prepared to work in the salt mines of passive nods, recognition of character assaults and desperate resignation, this gift will make real communication possible.

## THE ART OF DISCERNMENT

When managing schemas, which lie at the core of narcissism and dealing with a narcissist, discernment includes distinguishing between the here and now versus the "there and then". This is the gift of truth.

You communicate with a clarity that is based when you give discernment in the present moment.
You clear the past's cobwebbed barriers and join the domain of the present.
Without succumbing to it, you recognise history.
Like most of us, in your life, the narcissist is prone to allow the automatic nature of memory guides his truth. You can enable him to recognise reality in the present time and place from automatic beliefs and practices. Because you acknowledge the significance of paying attention and worked on this skill, you are prepared adroitly in your position as the wake-up caller.

**THE ART OF COLLABORATION**

Collaboration suggests mutual cooperation and invokes the power of "we". That's the offering of mutual effort.
Although we are all capable of making mistakes, in working together we also have something to give to each other.
Your dialogue is thoroughly carved from the philosophical clay of shared responsibility in a "we" state of communication.
You are informed by the extreme sensitivity of the narcissist to feel faulty and embarrassed, his fear of being taken advantage of, and his failure to ask for a connection.
You understand that when his schemas trigger those emotions, he may launch into a mode of entitlement, grandiosity, harassment, or avoidance. Since being collaborative keeps finger-pointing impulses under control, it helps keep the narcissist calm.
To mediate hierarchical struggles in treatment, cognitive psychologists and schema, therapists use "we" language with clients. This implies that we give our clients our knowledge and human experience in identifying emotions and connections between historical and current issues.
We assist them in creating strategies so that they can grasp, challenge, question and have input. We are not invested in power struggles. The objective of the cooperation is to foster

knowledge of the problems and to discover mutually agreeable solutions for change.

In particular, the cooperative strategy is essential with narcissists who are susceptible to buttoning up their vulnerability behind impermeable internal walls of self-protection.
While you cannot always imagine what will trigger you and the narcissist in your life, when you try to interact about how to enhance your connection with each other, you can artfully give the gift of the cooperative "we."

**THE ART OF ANTICIPATING CLASHES**

Anticipating clashes enables you to seize the anticipated traps in your relationship. This is the gift of foresight. This gift is provided in part by the biological makeup of the brain. You are endowed with the potential to attract upon memory to anticipate what lies ahead.
For instance, you may discover yourself finishing phrases for each other when you understand someone long enough and well enough. Or on the other hand what about your memory of the sharp twist in the road on your way to work? It's a memory that tells you to slow down originally and then accelerate into the turn to prevent losing your car's control. It is the wisdom of what-if and memory of how-to that keeps you secure.
We have an apparently infinite number of remembered experiences that enable us to prevent troubled encounters without even thinking about them.
Adding your enhanced care abilities to this already embedded gift, you have not just the wise intelligence of experience inside your grip, but a solid repertoire of on-the-spot reflexes. You can rebuild the very foundation on which your communications are based on your life's relationship with the narcissist.

**THE ART OF THE APOLOGY**

A sincere apology emphasises on the compassion for the wounded party, not the transgressor's redemption. This is the responsibility gift.
With this gift, you are responsible for the effects of your words, feelings and actions, particularly when they are hurtful. You know that your behaviour can be a model for how you want the narcissist to treat you, and you are hoping for reciprocity.
You are therefore modelling an apology based on a sympathetic knowledge of how and why certain messages hurt him in the hope that he will learn to give an apology that also represents an appreciation of your sensitivities. You convey genuinely remorseful emotions that are free from self-loathing and a self-centred concern with guilt. You are grounded in the other person's experience, not focused on a personal redemption mission. It's less about you than your responsibility.

**THE ART OF REFLECTIVE LISTENING**

Reflective listening includes mirroring another person's communication and extracting hidden feelings. This is the gift of balance.
You understand how to articulate information as well as how to set aside self-interest and invite your listener to speak to you. You are an ardent partner in communication that respectfully and patiently enables others to share themselves with trust, knowing that you will meet them without judgment.
You listen closely and reflect, without judgment, an unbiased replay of what you hear in an attempt to explain and validate. And while you may have a distinct point of perspective, you are waiting to convey it in your turn.
Being aware of how dangerous honest communication can be for the narcissist, you extract hidden meanings and masked

vulnerabilities by softly mirroring what you think stays unspoken.

You understand that you give the chance of mutual discovery by listening and reflecting.

Anything from the knowledge of a specific topic to managing contentious matters without being triggered, or from emotions about each other that have been locked in anger, apathy, or avoidance to a strength you never knew you had, or a realisation that the narcissist becomes receptive when he feels heard.

## CONCLUSION

This chapter explained seven gifts of effective communication in your lives with the narcissist and the interpersonal arts with which they are linked with.
If you use these arts to express yourself with integrity, from a flexible, open, receptive, skilled and enlightened state of mind, your own private FORCE is with you.

The artful implementation of the seven communication gifts will promote healthier, more pleasant, and more intimate relationships. And as you craft your speaking and listening with carefully selected words, voice tone, pacing, eye contact, facial expression, and body language, you will model what you want in exchange for these challenging interactions.
Having a voice that reflects you and your intentions correctly is always positive and to your advantage.
This has to be enough sometimes. In terms of changing someone else, there are no guarantees and no sure paths to victory. Typically, narcissists are not the kind of individuals who willingly seek help, coaching, or any assist in breaking down their impenetrable emotional boundaries. If anything, they avoid this sort of communication at almost all costs, whether through insistent rejection, mockery, externalising blame onto someone else, or different types of diversion and hiding.

That being said, you have learned how to play a crucial part in opening the door to the possibility of change, by leveraging if necessary, or perhaps simply by offering kindness and compassion. No matter what the outcome in reference to changes in the narcissist or your relationship with him, you can play an important part in your own liberation from fear, bullying, subjugation, self-sacrifice and even violence by recognising the life themes and schemas of your early experience, paying attention to triggering events and internal indications, setting boundaries and adjusting your reactions to both the narcissist and your own automatic internal dialogue. It may be the ultimate achievement to liberate this healthy, wise, and awakened self within you.

All of this book's approaches have the potential to be extremely efficient self-help methods to bring more satisfactory experiences with a narcissist. But the journey of self-help can be both isolated and arduous.
A professional therapist's assistance can sometimes be of tremendous value. Despite your best efforts, schemas can be very stiff and sometimes impenetrable.
I suggest that you should find someone versed in the foundations of cognitive-behavioural therapy and qualified in schema therapy if you choose to seek professional help.

# PART IX ESCAPING PERILOUS NARCISSISM

There are certain situations where a romantic relationship with a narcissist isn't worth battling for, even if you have the upper hand.
The narcissist possibly even be a fulmination to your (and your children's) security, safety, and stability. In the large majority of cases, these perilous narcissists are male.
Suggested explanations for the disparity include male temperament and greater inclination toward aggression, learned behaviours from primary male role models, social or cultural reinforcement, and biologically driven capabilities in reacting to stress and defeat when schemas are activated.

Dangerous narcissists never offer remorse, and in some instances, they show no signs of holding a moral compass.
In severe cases, their self-righteous rigidity may even mirror the traits of sociopaths; this type of narcissist often shows a complete disregard or contempt for others and for fundamental human experiences.
If you find yourself associated with such a narcissist, please contemplate making a safety plan to protect yourself and build an avenue for departure from the relationship.

# Identifying Dangerous Narcissism

Here are some typical behaviours of perilous narcissists.
Read through the following tables and carefully examine whether the narcissist in your life employs in these behaviours. Also, consider the regularity and degree to which he displays these behaviours.
If the narcissist in your life employs in just a few of these behaviours and only on occasion, it might be feasible to restore the relationship.
If, however, these behaviours are ubiquitous and pervasive, and particularly if they involve threats to your security, it's probably best to investigate a way out.

- Intimidations to Financial and Legal Security.
- Gambles unreasonably.
- Spends extravagantly.
- Feels entitled to drink and drive.
- Buys utilises or trades illicit drugs.
- Watches child pornography.
- Visits streetwalkers.
- Sidesteps taxes.
- Engages in nefarious and dishonest acts.
- Steals.
- Threats to Physical or Emotional Security.
- Engages in physically or verbally sadistic behaviour.
- Menaces to hurt you, your children, others, or possibly himself.
- Defames you and your children in public
- Damages property, tosses things, threatens to take the children or leave you poverty-stricken, or takes out his aggressiveness on pets.
- Declares on driving when under the influence of substances, even with you or your children in the vehicle.
- Threats to Security in Relationship and Society.

- Has affairs or engages in other promiscuous or risky intimate behaviour, including attending prostitutes or strip clubs or questionable viewing of
- pornography or attending adult chat rooms.
- Negligently exposes children to inappropriate material, language, or behaviours.
- Lies pathologically about virtually anything.
- Gets into fights with neighbours and other neighbourhood members.
- Doesn't display neighbourly behaviour despite notices from authorities, for example, pumping loud music, having no respect for the image of the property, or being noisy or exhibitionistic.

Because this profile is so prevalent, and because women often feel notable shame about revealing that their partner engages in such conduct, in this chapter, I'll focus on these sexual outlaws. If you're in a romantic relationship with a narcissist who is prone to physically threatening outbursts or behaviours that endanger your safety, please seek outside support immediately. Likewise, if the narcissist's behaviours display a genuine threat to your economic or legal security, I encourage you to form a plan to guard yourself and your children or remove yourself from the relationship, consulting a professional for assistance in this if need be.

## Constant justifications

Once identified, the narcissist typically rejects wrongdoing or attempts to minimise the damage.
He's usually prompt to offer the excuse that he's just like all men or to condemn his partner for being overweight, monotonous, rigid, or too preoccupied with the children, her job, or others. Keep in mind that his questionable behaviours

aren't the only way to deal with a feeling of isolation or sexual frustration.
Of course, the narcissist isn't expressly interested in hearing about how his
spouse feels anyway, much less chatting about the issue, observing his behaviour, or working on it.
And then there's that contention that this is just normal male sexuality.
For the entitled, narcissistic man, who is inept at tolerating feeling withdrawn or emotionally disturbed, this is the perfect rationalisation. How handy to be a member of a species in which he is awarded the absolute right to engage in sexual activity beyond his relationship. How convenient to pretend he has no say when it comes to the requests of his phallic emperor.
But consider this: If that were correct if his damaging sexual performances were just part of the male human condition, then why does he engage in them in secrecy, and why does he react with denial and accusing others when caught out?
That said, nature does perform a role in holding men's brains captive once they've entered this sexual territory.
Writer Roger Scruton points out that once people are driven by their porn obsession "to see sex in the instrumentalized way that pornography encourages, they begin to lose confidence in their ability to enjoy sex in any other way than through fantasy".

The brain can be enslaved by sexual stimulation, much like it reacts to sugar. Some of the data on brain function suggests that the addictive and stimulating rush of pleasure from pornography and other sexual activities outside of a partnership can dominate the satisfaction once found in the endorphin-releasing satisfaction of a sexual hiatus with one's partner.

This feeds into the coping behaviour of the narcissist, who has a deep-seated need to shut out his profoundly rooted pangs of loneliness and desolation—experiences he may see as boredom.

His search for disjoined self-stimulation when not engaged in other disturbances or holding court can lead him to seek out quick highs that ultimately may become enduring addictions, including sex addictions.

But this ravenous yearning for stimulation is a diversion from the underlying (and intolerable) emotional hunger he feels and that persists unnourished.

It doesn't hurt that so much of the easily available world of Internet pornography, telephone sex lines, and the like are intended to stroke the male ego, putting the narcissist on the plinth where he feels he belongs.

Plus, sexual rendezvous via pornography or with prostitutes need no intimacy, enabling the narcissist to get a quick fix with no mutuality required.

Given that narcissists aren't very good at giving back, how comfortable that there are no expectations put upon him, no one he must talk to or associate with authentically, and no one else's wants to consider. Even better, the object of his escape often pretends to find him absolutely enchanting and acts highly stimulated and excited by his "sexual intrepidity" and the size of his bulging…wallet. What an enticing treat for the unquenchable approval seeker.

**DECIDING WHETHER TO WALK AWAY**

In the case of dangerous narcissism, protection should be your first and foremost priority, especially if the narcissist's volatility, destruction, or threats are rising; if he is steadfast and un-remorseful in executing verbal or emotional abuse; or if he replies to your upset contemptuously or hatefully, beyond his chronic insolence and mistreatment of you.

Many women describe these unsafe behaviours as the most tragic and horrifying experiences in their relationship. Even if they use the most thoughtful idiom and most loving tone of voice in promoting peace for themselves and the welfare of the children, the dangerous narcissist may only grow more callous and menacing.

Again, this is a sign to put your security first and come up with an exit plan. But because so many narcissists can proceed to enrobe the Prince Charming mask even in these most challenging times, it can be tough to assess just how rooted their precarious behaviours are.

# Reforming the Average Narcissist

Fortunately, most narcissists don't fall into the dangerous category. If you're committed to staying in the relationship for whatever reason, or if you genuinely feel your partner is competent of change, you don't have to put up with continued violation. With expert help, the common narcissist usually apologises and pledges to change his conduct. He may even come to understand the impact of his sexual behaviour on you, your feelings toward him, and your sexual relationship. But without guidance, it's unlikely that such modifications will occur or endure. Rebuilding trust after a violation like this is a threefold attempt:
The exasperated partner must feel recognised.

The angry partner must figure out and obtain a way to communicate what she needs to feel secure—to trust again and reengage in affection.
The offended partner needs to feel secure enough to recognise the narcissist's changes and to acknowledge and applaud any manifestations of empathy he shows, whether requested or unrequested.
It may seem as if those three elements fall solely on the shoulders of the deceived partner. But a closer inspection exhibits that all three depend on the narcissist's dedication to change.
For you to feel appreciated, you must sense that your partner understands you—who you are at your core. To do this, he must determine to be empathically harmonised. He'll require help—someone to teach him abilities to avoid stumbling into automatic defensiveness and quick angry responses, which help him evade shameful "bad guy" feelings. Without these abilities, he will fail.
Besides, if you are to feel secure in communicating your needs and restoring trust, your partner must gain the courage to

plunge into the dark water and examine the sunken ship that houses his early struggles.

He must be prepared to look at how he developed his inclination to engage in addictive self-stimulating, and sequentially self-defeating, behaviours.

This is essential if he is to abundantly provide, without malice, the reassurance and clarity necessary for repairing trust.

This will also put him in a more favourable situation to share with you what drove him down this steep path, which will be precious in countering backsliding.

The third element—recognising the narcissist's changes and welcoming any signs of empathy—may appear the most difficult. Achieving this can feel like saying, "Everything's more normal now. You can go back to being as you were." Just recognise that your feelings of security are a requirement, and those feelings will only occur if the narcissist makes plentiful changes. He must also be patient and realise that your reentry into intimacy with him will be progressive. He must understand that your comfort level will grow and subside, especially when certain stimuli, such as the anniversary of a deception, trigger unpleasant emotions.

Finally, he must offer verbal reassurances in all of these concerns and continue to recognise and admit that he is liable for the rift among you. In time, you may recuperate and feel securely reattached to your self-worth, enabling you to be honest with him once anew—and perhaps eventually combine mutuality, kindness, and absolution into your relationship.

All of that may seem rather hard to imagine, and admittedly, it is uncommon. But with motivation, perseverance, and suitable leverage, it can transpire.

The recovery process isn't quick and yields many uncomfortable emotions to the surface: rage, grief, despair, and sadness enclosing a stained episode in a shared life story.

Couples involved in this process often ask how they can deal with the unpleasant truth of this element of their relationship. Once they progress beyond the acute stage of doubt, rage, and distress and have agreed upon a system for security and trust, I ask them to visualise a stunning architectural edifice. I point out that what customarily makes such structures eye-catching isn't flawlessly laid brick, one-dimensional colour, or highly refined stone, but flaws: abrasions in the brick, an assortment of colours, or weathered, rugged-edged rocks.

The group and its diversity are what make for vibrant and stunning architecture. These buildings have conquered the tests of time, of uncontrollable forces, and conceivably of war, and they have also been looked after by people who love them.

This is an appropriate metaphor for a lasting relationship: firm despite the difficulties to its infrastructure, rich with colours that represent both the brilliance and the pain, with some shortcomings that lend personality, and, most of all, painstakingly cared for by those who desire it to last.

If you and the narcissist have kids, love and worry for them can be a huge motivator for fighting hard to repair shattered trust and address the harm narcissism has wrought in your relationship.

Regrettably, out of their extreme necessity to feel safe, kids often assume the status of matrimonial referees. Don't put them in this situation or allow them to operate in this way.

And as you discovered in the first chapters, the consequences of narcissistic rage, entitlement, and belittlement on children can be quite damaging. Numerous kids simulate a narcissistic parent's behaviours and internalise that parent's manner of reasoning and communicating. Alternatively, children may take on problematical characteristics and coping methods of a non-narcissistic parent who is submissive, big-hearted, or fails to provide security.

## CONCLUSION

If you're in a romantic relationship with a precarious narcissist, I cannot stress enough the importance of guaranteeing your own protection and that of children, if you possess them. That said, the narcissist's intrepidity in utilising his charm can make it hard to ascertain whether he is truly unredeemable. Watch him firmly and mindfully—in the present moment and not through the lenses of your personal past experience. If you think you might reach through to him, and he may be able to change, use the conversation tactics in this book to try to engage the injured, disparaged person within. If you have a long-term relationship, this may be beneficial, as challenging as it may be.

If you choose to wait and attempt to restore the relationship, empathy will be one of your most efficient tools in cultivating change.

Made in United States
North Haven, CT
21 January 2022